# Early Services for Children with Special Needs

# Contents

# Early Services for Children with Special Needs

## Transactions for Family Support

### Second Edition

by

**Alfred Healy, M.D.**
**Patricia D. Keesee, M.S., CCC-SP**
**Barbara S. Smith, M.S.**
Iowa University Affiliated Program
Division of Developmental Disabilities
University Hospital School
The University of Iowa
Iowa City

·P·A·U·L·H·
BROOKES
PUBLISHING Cº

Baltimore • London • Toronto • Sydney

**Paul H. Brookes Publishing Co.**
Post Office Box 10624
Baltimore, Maryland 21285-0624

Typeset by Brushwood Graphics, Baltimore, Maryland.
Manufactured in the United States of America by
Thomson-Shore, Inc., Dexter, Michigan.

Cover design contributed by Loretta Popp.

**Library of Congress Cataloging-in-Publication Data**
Healy, Alfred, 1934–
   Early services for children with special needs.

   Includes bibliographies and index.
   1. Handicapped children—Services for—United States. 2.
Infants—Services for—United States. 3. Toddlers—Services for—
United States. I. Smith, Barbara, 1945–   . II. Keesee,
Patricia. III. Title.
HV888.5.H4  1988    362.4'048'088054    88-8118
ISBN 1-55766-012-3

# Introduction

Much has been learned over the last 25 years about service provision for very young at-risk and disabled children and about how the development of such children can be supported through special services. This growing knowledge is a result of both scientific research and the experience of practitioners and parents. The first edition of this book, originally published in 1985 under a grant from the Division of Maternal and Child Health, was intended to help strengthen the link between the knowledge base and what is actually practiced in early intervention programs. This second edition seeks to achieve the same goal by addressing these broad questions:

What is known about at-risk and disabled children and their families that should influence our efforts to meet their special needs?
What are the barriers to translating this knowledge into program practices?
What concrete steps can be taken to improve this translation process?

The purpose of this second edition of the book is to focus these questions more closely on the *mission* and specific *mandates* that have been solidified by the passage of Public Law 99-457, the Education of the Handicapped Act Amendments of 1986. This legislation made a giant step toward translating knowledge about early development into public policy. Its dramatic focus on support for the family as a means of enhancing the development of the child, and its concentration on interdisciplinary and interagency efforts to plan and carry out services, bring new hope for the future of some of our most vulnerable citizens. PL 99-457 has also made a common base of understanding all the more important because of the new participants who are involved in the implementation of this bill. The need for an expression of policies and practices that support quality services, in a language that can be readily understood by the wide variety of participants in this process, seems even more vital than it did in 1985.

Our intended audience, then, should include the broad range of individuals specified as participants in the law's implementation. For some of these individuals, particularly for those residing in states that have previously not been heavily involved in early services, this may be a relatively new area. These participants include members of lead agencies designated in each state and the interagency coordinating council members who will be assisting the lead agency. Included are parents, providers, legislators, agency representatives involved in payment of services, and people involved in personnel preparation.

In addition, we hope to reach the practitioners in community settings who may not be familiar with national issues or with the thinking of national leaders. The book may be useful as a component of programs for students in areas such as early childhood special education, physical therapy and occupational therapy, speech-language pathology and audiology, medicine, social work, and psychology. Parents who want to learn more about early intervention and issues in service organization may find this work helpful. We also hope that people involved in planning new community or state programs, or those wishing to improve existing programs, will find some direction here.

The concepts presented in this work are unlikely to appear new or bold to those familiar with early intervention services. However, our approach was based on the belief that many of these concepts have been accepted and incorporated into the service jargon without addressing the changes needed in services to make these concepts a reality. For example, the concept of *parental involvement* is widely accepted, even mandated, but it has not always been translated into practice. The term is variously defined by different programs, and by different professionals within a given program. Program goals and practices of specific disciplines often do not take parental involvement into consideration and can even prohibit it. While the new legislation is a bold step toward clarifying the mission, it cannot sweep away these discrepancies. This work provides a framework for looking at such discrepancies and some beginning steps for dealing with them.

## LITERATURE

One aspect of our consensus was to review the literature of special relevance to early services for very young at-risk and disabled children and their families. Both annotated and unannotated categorized bibliographies accompany this text. We have included texts that date predominantly from the 1980s, and also periodicals dating from 1983 to the present. However, numerous exceptions have been made in order to cite earlier publications that have promoted growth in the field of early intervention services for at-risk and disabled children and their families. In order to avoid the complexities of a historical review, but to present current "consensus," we have assumed that the most important work prior to these dates is accounted for through associated references in the newer works. References were chosen for annotation primarily because they provide relatively direct access to pivotal concepts and issues in the field of early intervention for practitioners and students. They have been judged by the present authors to be particularly clear representations of current thought. The unannotated references guide the reader to literature that additionally reflects major themes and significant trends in theory, and investigative activity of importance in early services for very young children and their families.

We have also chosen not to use point-to-point citations in the text. Extensive citations of every major point would be required and undoubtedly some important contributions would be missed. We also felt that a major goal of producing this readable summary of themes would be better achieved without traditional research citations. To compensate for this unconventional approach, the bibliographies demonstrate the scope of our review. We hope the bibliographies will serve as a useful resource for readers as well as an alternative to text citations.

## CONTRIBUTORS

A major effort of our consensus gathering project was listening to professionals and parents who are involved intimately with service issues. Although contributors to this project came from widely varying backgrounds, their statements identifying the key issues in early intervention and the barriers to improved services were strikingly similar. The answers to our question: *"What have you learned in your work that is most relevant to how and what services should be available for at-risk and disabled children"?* were not answers that were tied directly to the respondent's particular area of expertise. Instead, they encompassed practical humanistic concerns relevant to all disciplines involved with the very young child. In drawing their answers together, we want to emphasize the importance of the family environment, the need for individualized services, and the need for the consistent use of trained observation and quality interdisciplinary decision making in all aspects of programming.

Our first efforts in this project were accomplished through our formal relationship with six consultants. These consultants included Leonard W. Hall, Ph.D., then Executive Director of the American Association of University Affiliated Programs, representing educational issues; Lewis P. Lipsitt, Ph.D., Director of the Child Study Center at Brown University, representing child development issues; Charles S. Mahan, M.D., Director of Maternal and Child Health in the state of Florida, representing obstetrical concerns; Stephanie H. Porter, R.N., parent specialist at Project Welcome in Boston, and the mother of a premature infant, representing parent concerns; Emily Schrag, M.S.W., Associate Director for Publications and Public Policy at the National Center for Clinical Infant Programs in Washington, D.C., representing public policy issues; and Jack P. Shonkoff, M.D., Co-Director of the Child Development Service at the University of Massachusetts Medical Center in Worcester, representing developmental pediatrics and health. The principal themes evolved not only from our contacts with these consultants individually, but also through their interaction with each other and with practitioners and parents who have also met with them.

Another contribution to the consensus was a formal review of our efforts by 11 professionals of national reputation who had the opportunity to critique and make additions to the text. Contributors were chosen to represent the wide range of disciplines and issues involved with early intervention, and included: John A. Butler, Ed.D., Principal Investigator for the Collaborative Study of Children with Special Needs at Children's Hospital Medical Center, Boston, representing health planning and public health; Suzann K. Campbell, Ph.D., P.T., Professor in the Division of Physical Therapy at the University of North Carolina at Chapel Hill; Juanita W. Fleming, R.N., Ph.D., F.A.A.N., Associate Dean and Director of Graduate Education at the University of Kentucky, representing nursing concerns; H.D. Bud Fredericks, Ph.D., Associate Director of the Teaching Research Division of Western Oregon State College, representing early childhood special education; Elnora M. Gilfoyle, D.Sc., O.T.R., F.A.O.T.A., Associate Professor and head of the Department of Occupational Therapy at Colorado State University; Alex Gitterman, M.S.W., Ph.D., Associate Dean of Social Work at Columbia University; Bea Gold, M.A., Director of Children, Youth, and Family Services, in Los Angeles, representing interdisciplinary interests and early childhood; Robert J. Harmon, M.D., Director of the Infant Psychiatry Clinic at the University of Colorado Health Science Center, representing infant mental health issues; Fern and Joe Kupfer of Ames, Iowa, representing parent interests and advocacy; Rose Ann Langham, R.D., Dr.P.H., Administrator of the nutrition section of the Louisiana Department of Health and Human Resources; and Arthur H. Parmelee, M.D., Head of the Division of Child Development, Department of Pediatrics, University of California School of Medicine, Los Angeles.

It has been our intent from the beginning to create a document that would be useful to community practitioners in early intervention programs. To ensure this, the project held three regional forums at university affiliated facility sites at the University of California, Irvine, the University of Kansas Medical Center, Kansas City, and Georgetown University, Washington, DC. The participants at each forum (identified in the Acknowledgments) were carefully chosen to represent parents and grassroots practitioners, including administrators, health care professionals, social workers, teachers, and therapists in early intervention programs. Using an early draft of the text as a starting point, the day-long discussions covered a range of topics organized to gather the experiences of the participants and their thoughts about how improvements could be made in early intervention practices. Broadly, we focused on two questions: 1) did the draft document accurately reflect the issues involved in working on behalf of at-risk and disabled children ages birth to three? 2) If so, by what processes could statements in the draft document be practically implemented in community programs?

The forums were a gratifying and enlightening experience. The issues described in the text were confirmed as being of central importance in the day-to-day functioning of practitioners and parents, and our approach to bringing the issues together was well received. At the same time, we developed a much stronger sense of the practical challenges represented by these issues. The anecdotes added as a result of the forums describe the challenges, as well as the commitment and sensitivity of the practitioners and parents.

## SOCIOECONOMIC RISK

Early intervention services were first developed for children who were at risk for socioeconomic reasons. Later, services were included to prevent, ameliorate, or help compensate for disabilities. One cannot deal in even a cursory fashion with studies related to the biologically at-risk or disabled child without noting the powerful relationship between socioeconomic status and any outcome indices, whether related to child development or family adjustment. In addition, we know that the incidence of some risk factors—prematurity, for example—is higher in lower socioeconomic environments.

We have not attempted in this text to clearly separate the population of biologically at-risk children from those who are environmentally or socioeconomically at risk. The need for interdisciplinary services and interagency collaboration, and the issues of family-centered services, are relevant regardless of the nature of the risk factors involved. Public Law 99-457, while not requiring that states include at-risk children in their early intervention system, clearly recognizes the importance of that option. No one is immune from the tragic surprise of disability. The question: *"Why has this happened to us?"* comes in all languages, and from all cultural backgrounds and income levels. The new law is for everyone. But at the same time, we hope it will help move national policy toward a recognition that statistically, the factor most predictive of problems for children, in health or in almost any aspect of their development, is *poverty*.

## CHAPTER ORGANIZATION

Chapters have been organized around areas of concern to the professionals and parents involved with at-risk and disabled children. Each chapter outlines the themes that have emerged from research and experience, and the possible interpretations and implications of these themes for implementing responsive community services, and for carrying out PL 99-457. These areas include: 1) child development as it relates to the special needs of the at-risk and disabled child, 2) parent-professional interactions, 3) developmental programs, 4) social attitudes and policies, 5) the elements of service delivery organization, and 6) action steps for implementation.

We offer this work as a contribution to the vital national effort that has been galvanized by Public Law 99-457, and as a guide to indicate areas where future efforts can be constructively focused.

# Acknowledgments

In the course of working on this project, the list of persons to whom the authors are indebted has accumulated to a directory-like collection. While we present this indebtedness as lists of names, without exception, the individuals provided not only specific disciplinary contributions, but also personal support and enthusiasm, for which we are enormously grateful. The cooperation of all meant that the project was a truly interdisciplinary effort.

Our first note of thanks goes to the Division of Maternal and Child Health, U.S. Department of Health and Human Services, for their financial support and encouragement in developing the first edition of this book. Specifically, we are grateful for reviews and concrete advice from Merle McPherson, M.D., Chief of the Division. We are also grateful to the National Center for Clinical Infant Programs in Washington, D.C., for collaboration in identifying professionals for the consulting and review process.

Our six national consultants and eleven reviewers played a major role in identifying the issues of concern and how to approach them, and we are most appreciative of their efforts. Their names and the roles they played in the consensus process are referenced in the Introduction.

The planning and conduct of the three regional forums involved extensive cooperative planning between our staff and university affiliated program staff at the University of California, Irvine, the University of Kansas Medical Center, and Georgetown University Hospital, Washington, DC. These UAP contacts were responsible for finding the designated representation of parents and practitioners for the forums, as well as for the mechanics of the day-long meetings. Thanks to the efforts of the UAP staff, our goals for these events were more than met. Their moral support and hospitality were appreciated by all.

The forum participants, while highly individual in experience and personality, were uniformly outstanding group participants. Forum discussions were candid and, through a full day of discussion, participant energy levels remained high and well focused. While we have not identified the speakers in material quoted, we have distinct and warm impressions of each participant in our working memory. Following are the individuals involved with the three forums:

## UNIVERSITY OF CALIFORNIA, IRVINE

### Department of Pediatrics

*University Affiliated Facility Staff:* Kenneth W. Dumars, M.D., Director; Deborah Duran-Flores, M.S.Ed., O.T.R. *Forum participants:* Mary Lou Again, R.N., P.H.N., Orange, CA; Carmian Atchley (parent), Anaheim, CA; Mary Lou Bayle, speech-language pathologist, Buena Park, CA; Sue Cue, O.T.R., Santa Ana, CA; Rosemary Ford, M.S., M.S.W., Cerritos, CA; Mary Grant, P.T., Irvine, CA; Steve Green, M.S., C.C.C.-S.P., Orange, CA; Joan Hess, R.N., P.H.N., Anaheim, CA; Mary Lou Hickman, M.D., Sacramento, CA; Kathy Lopez (parent), Garden Grove, CA; Doug McDougall, M.A. (administrator), Los Angeles, CA; Susan Zwilling, M.S., O.T.R., Laguna Beach, CA.

## UNIVERSITY OF KANSAS MEDICAL CENTER, KANSAS CITY

### Children's Rehabilitation Unit

*University Affiliated Facility Staff:* Jane Rues, Ed.D., Acting Director. *Forum participants:* Dave Bennett, Ph.D. (administrator), Kansas City, MO; Linda Benton, M.S., O.T.R., Topeka, KS; Holly Buser, R.P.T., Kansas City, MO; Cindy Fieser, R.N., Kansas City, MO; Glenda Figge (parent), Kansas City, KS; Russ Hedge, M.A. (administrator), Parsons, KS; Grace Holmes, M.D., Kansas City, KS; Mary Jo Janose, R.P.T., Independence, MO; Fran Kokrda, M.S. (educator), Shawnee Mission, KS; Elvira Ramirez, A.C.S.W., Kansas City, KS; Jean Bailey-Smith, M.S.W., Kansas City, MO; Kristi Smith-Wyatt (parent), Kansas City, MO.

## GEORGETOWN UNIVERSITY HOSPITAL, WASHINGTON, DC

### Child Development Center

*University Affiliated Facility Staff:* Phyllis R. Magrab, Ph.D., Director; Elliot Gersh, M.D.; Kathy Katz, Ph.D.; Donna Deardorff. *Forum participants:* Edwinna Albergottie, M.S.W., A.C.S.W., Washington, DC; Charlene Booker (parent), Washington, DC; Marcia Cain Coling, M.A. (educator), Bethesda, MD; Martine Ehrenreich, L.P.T., Wheaton, MD; Barbara Fleming (parent), Alexandria, VA; June Gagnon, Ph.D. (administrator), Upper Marlboro, MD; Jacqueline McMorris, M.D., Washington, DC; Sabrina Schulze, M.S.W., Washington, DC; Jane Stanga, M.A. (educator), Arlington, VA.

In addition to our national contacts, we relied on Iowa resources to help identify issues and critique drafts of the text. We invited parents and professionals at different times to meet with our consultants, to review text, and to discuss specific issues with us. These contacts included: Charles Betts, parent advocate; James Blackman, M.D., pediatrician; Michael Bonato, urban and regional planner; Mary Ellen Becker, speech-language pathologist; Diane Garber, parent/infant educator; Carla Lawson, parent advocate; Peg Maher, hearing clinician; Mary McCue, social worker; Ann Riley, R.N. and day-care provider; Ernie Scheeler, social worker; David Schor, M.D., pediatrician; Matthew Sell, M.D., neonatologist; and Anne Steffensmeier, speech-language pathologist. In addition, Herman A. Hein, M.D., director of the Iowa Perinatal Care Program, and Reid Zehrbach, Ph.D., supervisor of the Early Childhood Program, Grant Wood Area Education Agency, served as our local project advisors.

And finally, we offer heartfelt thanks to our project staff at the Division of Developmental Disabilities. Editorial assistance has been ably supplied by Susan B. Eberly. Christopher C. Green and MariAnne P. Ryan worked with great determination on the bibliographies. Design artist Loretta Popp has contributed her talents to graphic issues. Suzanne M. Switzer and Nancy A. Bradshaw have been bedrocks of competence, patience, and good cheer since the very beginning—kind friends.

To all these persons and to the many others who have offered their informal assistance along the way, we extend thanks for sharing our concern with the issues presented in this text.

# Early Services for Children with Special Needs

# Chapter 1

# Early Intervention
## Themes for Services

This chapter will present key issues regarding:

- **family support and the nature of early intervention**
- **parental empowerment and parental involvement**
- **the science of early intervention**
- **service organization**
- **training**

Early intervention services are educational, health, and social services designed to support the development of very young children who, in minor or major ways, have been identified as "different." They are also designed to support and strengthen the families that are the primary influence on these children. Whether a child's differentness involves medical fragility, an identifiable disabling condition, or membership in a "high-risk" group such as premature infants, parents and professionals have urgent concerns about doing the right thing at the right time.

These concerns have now been translated into a national mandate through Public Law 99-457, Part H, the Education of the Handicapped Amendments of 1986. The mandate outlines 14 minimum requirements for implementing a comprehensive early intervention system that will promote the development of at-risk or disabled young children. States, over the course of the implementation process, must develop or identify the following:

1. A definition of developmental delay
2. A timetable for availability of services
3. A comprehensive multidisciplinary evaluation of the needs of children and families
4. An individualized family service plan that includes case management services
5. A child-find and referral system
6. A public awareness program to focus on early identification
7. A central directory of services, resources, state experts, research, and demonstration projects
8. A comprehensive system of personnel development
9. A single line of authority to a lead agency
10. A policy for contracting or making arrangements with local service providers
11. A procedure for timely reimbursement of funds
12. Procedural safeguards
13. Policies and procedures for personnel standards
14. A system for compiling data regarding the early intervention program

Whether states have existing early intervention programs or whether they will be starting from the beginning, there is a need for a useful summary of philosophies and knowledge gathered from research and experience. This book is an effort to provide such a summary. As a whole, we focus on these questions:

What has been learned about at-risk and disabled children and their families that should influence our efforts to meet their special needs?
What are the barriers to translating this knowledge into program practices?

What concrete steps can be taken to improve this translation process?

This first chapter deals with some of the major issues that are of current concern in the field of early intervention services. Issues can be defined as points of debate or controversy: matters that are yet unsettled. From our review, it appears that there are certain key issues that must be confronted and resolved if early intervention services are to be responsive to the needs of children and families, and if state systems are to be responsive to PL 99-457. These issues involve points of philosophy and social policy as well as points of science. In Chapters 2 through 6, these issues reappear thematically in the specific topics of early development, parent-professional interactions, developmental programs, social policy, and service organization. Chapter 7 presents an outline of steps for addressing the issues that are consistent with PL 99-457.

## FAMILY SUPPORT AND THE NATURE OF EARLY INTERVENTION

A therapist reports: "The parents may be doing okay until the kid is identified as having a problem, even though the child hasn't changed one bit from Monday when he didn't have this problem to Tuesday when we said he did. I had a parent say to me one time in great distress: 'Early intervention is intrusive.' And I said: 'Yes, it is.' He said: 'If my son were normal, you wouldn't be coming here watching me feed him.' I said: 'You're absolutely right.' "

Early intervention by its nature is an intimate service that touches a family's life at a time of double vulnerability. First, there is the normal vulnerability of a family taking on responsibility for a first or additional child. Second, there is the often dramatic vulnerability brought on by the special needs situation. These vulnerabilities may complicate already existing problems, such as low socioeconomic status, unemployment, marital stress, or teenage parenthood.

Concerns over the use of the expression *early intervention*

reflect important issues in the delivery of services. Some professionals express concern that the term suggests a cure, thus encouraging false hopes that intervention could halt the disability
itself. Others are uneasy about the authoritarian tone of the term
*intervention,* which is not compatible with the kind of gentle,
family-centered approach that should be part of these services.
In some cases, what is done for the infant or young child does in
fact come between the infant and his or her family or environment, as in the case of direct medical procedures or direct physical or environmental manipulations. When the term is applied to
activities designed to promote normal attachment and interaction between caregivers and the child with special needs, it seems
less applicable and even misleading. While we will continue to
use the term, it is intended to imply support rather than intervention.

While all that we have learned about child development
and service delivery to this special population points to the fact
that the family environment is overall *the* most critical variable
in predicting a child's outcome, the relative balance of a family-
support versus child-centered focus for early intervention services has not been well articulated or resolved for most individual practitioners, let alone for programs.

One aspect of this issue is that family support can be
broadly defined to include a wide variety of functions. At a basic
level in the hierarchy of needs, it can involve helping families obtain food stamps, housing, Medicaid, employment, or other ne-
cessities of life. Family support also encompasses counseling parents about the child's disabling condition, helping parents to find
services or become case managers, and directing them to sources
of information about their child's condition. It can also include
the provision of emotional support in a variety of ways, including informal parent-professional friendships, formal counseling,
and arranging visits with other parents in similar situations.

The issue of what family support means is one that will be
central to the development of the Individualized Family Service
Plan (IFSP) called for in the new legislation. While most professionals would agree that all of these aspects of family support are
important for at least some of the families they work with, there

is some frustration and disagreement over what family support encompasses for a particular service or professional discipline. "We've been talking a lot about this very question," says one therapist. "We don't do enough for families. We say we use a family-centered rather than a child-centered model, and then we say well, no, we really do not. We don't really do that much. How can we do more"? A therapist in a hospital-based program comments: "You either have to choose to support the family or support the child. I guess you could kind of split it. But for me it's hands on; the child is first, the therapy is first. That's my personal bias. If I had some extra staff, we could probably do more things for the family."

Underlying the new legislation is the strong belief that it is not possible to serve the child well without considering a variety of family support efforts. Services that center on family support can present significant staffing and administrative problems. It is, according to one administrator: "a very inconvenient concept." "We try to follow through and guide families to agencies that can help them," reports a pediatrician in a developmental clinic, "but some of these mothers need someone to take them by the hand and actually take them there. We've done that, but sporadically. We don't have the staff to build that kind of follow-through into our program." "It was always easier for me to make the decision to get involved with family support when a child had very little potential or was perhaps dying," commented a therapist. "Then I knew my therapeutic intervention wasn't going to do very much."

Despite the legislation's strong commitment to the family, it will still be complicated to fund some kinds of family support efforts. According to one professional: "In our program the parent is not considered a client, only the child, and you can't deal with the parameters that are not child-centered and expect acknowledgment or remuneration for it. We need to define family support in terms more acceptable to policy makers and still get the essence of what we all know we want to have for these families."

Many professionals feel that a family support orientation is critical for the practice of their own disciplines. A therapist reports: "I have to support the family. If I have a child who has a feeding problem, I'm not really very effective unless I can work with the family and help them be more competent, the mother and father, as caregivers."

One social worker provides evidence that this effectiveness can be translated into administrative understanding and financial success. "I work for a private company that deals with in-home nursing services for handicapped children. My administrators are now very receptive to my working with families and supporting families, and they pick up these costs. They find that cases go more smoothly, that it actually makes good business sense. And the families spread the word that this service has worked well for them, so it's good for public relations as well."

"Particularly, legislators need to learn about the long-term cost benefits of supporting families," says a nurse, "that it leads to increased competence and fewer demands on the system down the road. In England, where it is the expectation to have family support services, politicians won't get elected unless they are behind the idea."

The rationale for and the barriers to family support services are dealt with in more detail in later chapters, particularly in the chapters on parent-professional interactions and on social attitudes and policy. It is clear that family support in some or all of its definitions is an important part of early intervention. People in early intervention programs need to know how family support will be defined and how resources will be used to make it possible.

## FAMILY EMPOWERMENT AND PARENT PARTICIPATION

Another issue of concern to practicing professionals that is closely tied to family support and to early intervention program planners involves the relationship between parents or other family members and professionals, and the role each plays in early intervention services. While we refer in this book primarily to parents, we include in that term other family or nonfamily members who fulfill significant caregiving roles for the child. This issue may take the form of a number of important questions: What role should parents play in actual therapies? What is successful parent-professional collaboration? What is the professional's role in helping build parental competence? How can parent-professional communications be monitored to ensure the "openness" that is needed?

Early intervention comes at the beginning of what for some parents will be a long period of contact with professionals regarding their child. For most parents of at-risk or disabled children, this beginning stage is a difficult one.

---

**"I know when you find out you have a handicapped child—at least my reaction was that I felt totally out of control," reports one mother, "and at the very beginning, I felt I was powerless, that I had to take the word of every professional that we had to deal with because I didn't know anything. Gradually, I began to feel that I wasn't so out of control, that I did have some power, given my limitations. You *can* learn things and make wise decisions as you gain confidence and experience. Parents have to realize that they can have this power."**

---

Some professionals and parents object to the use of the term *empowerment* because it implies that professionals are "giving" parents power that, by right, is already theirs. But most parents do in fact initially have feelings of powerlessness. Professionals can cultivate those negative feelings by encouraging dependence, or, conversely, they can be part of the process of helping the parent move from a state of shock-induced passivity to one of mobilization. Professionals do not give power to parents, but they can facilitate and nurture parental self-assurance; early intervention services should encourage this process. Programs must ask, then, "How do we do this?" and: "How do we know when we are successful?"

"To me," remarked one practitioner, "it seems like our problems come from not deciding what our attitude is in the first place. It comes from the whole staff not having a particular philosophy in their approach to parents. Some professionals feel threatened by parents. They don't want them in individual therapy; they see them as 'others,' not as partners. If I were consulting for a new program, I would say: 'Sit down and decide what your philosophy is in dealing with parents first, and then the structure will just kind of fall in place, and you can monitor each other and the parents can monitor you, too.' "

The issue of parental participation in early intervention is in a sense a sub-issue of the area of parental empowerment. Questions such as whether or not parents will administer therapy, or become case managers, directly relate to how much power they feel they have and how well they can sort through what is best for themselves and for their child. Often, parental participation is invoked through formal processes. "One of my pet peeves," says an administrator, "is the whole Individual Habilitation Plan (IHP) or Individualized Education Program (IEP) process. These meetings, where there are maybe eight professionals in a room with the parents, are mandated, and we wonder why the parents' attendance is poor. We all know this is a problem and yet it goes on year after year . . ."

In the development of the family plan, the IFSP that is called for in PL 99-457, there is a great desire on the part of both professionals and parents to avoid these kinds of problems.

A social worker comments: "Think of participation as a kind of cognitive map. That map can be as elaborate as the parents are capable of handling . . . as they learn one part, you may add another part." "I have a real hard time with involving parents as *case managers*," offers another. "I'm thinking—this is just being a parent. Let the parent be a parent. You've heard about this program or this doctor; you can decide where your child will go, just the way parents of normal children do. It's a normal process and we make it sound real abnormal by calling it *case management.*"

Resolving the issues surrounding the relationship between parents and professionals in early intervention programs is an important aspect of service improvement. These issues are explored more fully in Chapter 3.

## THE SCIENCE OF EARLY INTERVENTION

A third major issue in the practice of early intervention concerns its role as a scientific effort. Early intervention is based on assumptions about when and how learning occurs, about the importance of early experience to later development, and on the hypothesis that the activities of early intervention have "good effects" on the child and family. In order to be effective, early intervention must possess certain characteristics. First, science and service in this area must be closely aligned to provide careful observation of the child and of the effects of interventions. Second, there must be well-defined terminology by which observations can be shared. Third, measures of efficacy are needed that can report, over the short and the long run, whether intervention efforts do in fact have positive effects. These are all elements of the scientific mission of early intervention. PL 99-457 calls for statewide centralized collection of data on children served and programs available; this will offer great opportunities for monitoring system effectiveness in a more scientific way. The issue that programs themselves must deal with, then, is how to keep science alive in day-to-day practice.

Observation is the core of scientific activity, and it can be lost in the routine demands of service delivery. Observation is the key to determining what practices should be attempted with a particular individual. Thus, observation of the child and of the effects of intervention efforts should be an integral part of practice. The sharing of these observations between clinical practitioners and the formal research community is a critical part of improving early intervention services as well.

Lack of meaningful training experiences and restrictions

of staff time are major barriers to emphasizing observation in early intervention practice. Careful observation is both difficult and time consuming; for the many professionals who spend years learning techniques to use with children, observation may be a step that is easy to drop. "They can have an appointment with the mother of a preemie," reports one nurse, "and some therapists already feel they know the answer, know what they will do before they even meet the mother. They come with the solution and don't know the problem." A nurse who took an inservice course specifically designed to promote observational skills reports on a change in her approach to her work: "Now I feel like I'm taking more time to sit back and observe, rather than just constantly having my wheels turning, and saying I could do this for that." A speech-language pathologist says: "I don't think enough emphasis is put on the quality of observations in training programs. Most of the students would come to their observational 'obligations' and say: 'Oh no, I have to do observation hours.' Now, I'd love to go back and observe and really learn something from it."

A pediatrician supervising medical residents in a developmental clinic supports the need for careful observation. "Child development is 100% observation: observing the child, the family. I have a real hard time with my students sometimes because they're really caught up in *doing,* and I have to take them out of the room and put them in an observation booth where they can't get their hands on anyone and they can't talk. I mean, if you put them in a room with a parent, they feel obligated to say something and I just cringe because there's not enough quiet observing time. They say too much. When they review their rotations in child development, they say: 'We didn't do anything,' and they downgrade us because we have them observing. They feel like if they don't do it with their hands on, then they haven't learned anything. It's very difficult to convince people that observing is important. They want to learn to do procedures."

Few training programs have emphasized "quiet" observation, and the observation techniques that *are* promoted are hard to maintain once the practitioner is actually working in the field. "When I first worked in neonatology, it was under a grant," reports an occupational therapist, "and I was able to observe for 8 months in the unit before I really ever touched anyone. But that's not very cost-effective. It's not the real world." "With new contracts and insurance programs it is increasingly difficult to have time to observe in any kind of clinical setting," reports an administrator. "That is a real barrier to overcome. You have to be productive and pay your way in the clinic setting, and the role of observation in your work is not part of that payment system." Ways of building observation into program methods, and ways to help parents become good observers, are clearly areas that need attention.

Observations, interventions, and goals must be tied to well-defined terminology if experience is to be effectively shared between professionals, between programs, between parents and professionals, or between researchers and practitioners. We have already discussed the need to define such broadly used terms as *family support* and *parental involvement*. States are also asked to carefully define the populations they will serve under PL 99-457, and to indicate how they will define developmental delay. The specifics of various practices need to be carefully defined as well. "Everyone is on the bandwagon saying: 'Let's do infant stim.,' " says a neonatal nurse. "They slap a picture up on the wall of the incubator and leave it there for 6 months. That's not stimulation. Let's figure out what we're talking about."

The science of early intervention also calls for well-established goals for services, and efficacy measures related to those goals. Without these two elements in place, the sharing of successes and improvement in services will be impossible. Traditionally, measures of program efficacy have been related to cognitive development in the child. For example, how many IQ points can be raised as a result of intervention? "We're stuck on the numbers," a social worker says. "I can sit down with a family and the numbers show no gains, but qualitatively the family feels good, is pleased with the child's interactive abilities. You have to really look at a different level, and none of the standardized tests pick up on that qualitative aspect of children's development." "I have a different perspective on goals than many people new to the field," says one experienced teacher. "I started working with older children. I was still stacking blocks with 16-year-olds. It doesn't look so bad when you do that with a 12-month-old, but the parents kept saying: 'Where is this getting us?' and I gave them answers but, hey, I didn't know where it was getting us either. It didn't matter whether this kid could stack blocks or not, she was just not getting anywhere. When we work with very young children we have to ask this too: 'What *are* our goals? What do we want here? What is important?' "

Efficacy studies have not clearly supported the notion that early intervention will consistently elevate cognitive levels for the population of at-risk and disabled children. If early intervention is to become more concerned with issues that relate to child and family adjustment to disability, to coping skills, and to functioning in the world, measures of efficacy must be developed that relate to these goals. Chapter 2 and Chapter 4 deal more extensively with these issues.

## SERVICE ORGANIZATION

When children need services that involve professionals from many disciplines and from multiple agencies, the goal should be to have services that are accessible, so the family does not have the added burden of dealing with a confusing service delivery system.

In line with current thinking on how services can be delivered most effectively, PL 99-457 calls for services to be multidisciplinary. Furthermore, there should be interagency coordination, and, as much as possible, services should be community based. Also, case management services should be provided for families. Many would agree with the desirability of these concepts, but their definition and the practicalities involved in carrying them out present important issues for programs and for individual practitioners. For example, practitioners need to know how interdisciplinary function should be defined and structured for individual programs. Additionally, how can the coordination of services across agency lines be best accomplished? Who determines criteria for access to programs?

Interdisciplinary function involves encouraging professionals to surrender some of their "turf," and to share decision making in the best interests of a child and family. There are many practical difficulties in communication between people who may not be working together all the time. "My son was having surgery," reports one mother, "and both a plastic surgeon and an orthopedic surgeon were going to be involved at the same time. I asked: 'Can't we get the two of you together and discuss the pros and cons?' They both said: 'It's impossible for us to schedule a time to meet together with you.' " I said: 'Well, you're doing it for the surgery aren't you?' Then one said: 'I see your point. I'll try to arrange it.' " "If everyone were housed in the same building it would be okay," reports a therapist. "But we have to communicate by phone and reports. You leave a message. He calls back and you aren't there. It goes back and forth. Paperwork takes forever, back and forth. It becomes very frustrating. It isn't the best definition of *interdisciplinary*."

Poor interagency communication can present significant problems for parents. Barriers to effective interagency cooperation can result when staff are overburdened, but interagency competition for children and funds can also hinder cooperation. "Interagency cooperation is much more of a problem than interdisciplinary cooperation," says one therapist. "One particular agency I know actually had a policy of noncooperation. It was amazing. They wouldn't let us see their IEPs. They didn't want ours. The teacher and I did it all under the table. But officially we could never meet. We were not allowed to meet."

Criteria for access to programs, and the availability of specific programs, are additional examples of serious organizational concerns confronting parents. "There are programs that want kids to be 2 calendar years delayed before they will be admitted," offers a speech pathologist. "When we're talking about kids from birth to 3, that's tough. Too many kids and not enough slots, so they set up these impossible criteria." "I serve a population in two counties," says a nurse, "and one of my big concerns is the inequity of services based on where you live. Families in one county get services, and just over the line they don't unless they have a whole lot of money of their own." Some children don't get access to programs because they are too mildly involved, others because they are too severely involved. "Two parents in our support group have kids that nobody wanted," says a social worker. "They were given funding for physical therapy for 6 months. It didn't do any good, so they were dropped. The parents said everyone gave up on them. They were ineligible for services because it was determined that the kids had no rehabilitation potential. So what are the parents going to do with them?"

The issues arising from the organization of service delivery are complex, and involve questions of funding, as well as professional and agency "turf" problems. The focus must be on the needs of the families as organizational problems are addressed. These issues are covered more fully in Chapter 5 and Chapter 6.

## TRAINING

Many of the issues related to improving early intervention services are at least in part related to preservice and inservice training, which is why PL 99-457 calls for states to develop personnel standards and a comprehensive plan for personnel development. Concerns over training do not relate primarily to the teaching of disciplinary skills, but to the imparting of attitudes and skills related to observations and interdisciplinary decision making. Sensitivity, communication, and respect for families are also related.

The timing of training efforts is clearly a critical issue. "I find the first year of residency is not the time to push some of these qualitative issues," reports a pediatrician. "The first-year residents are quite sure they have things well in hand. After a year, they have had enough experiences where their medical knowledge was not enough and they say: 'My God, I don't have so much power after all.' They begin to see they don't have that much control and they can listen to other people." "We had doctorate level graduate students in psychology," reports another clinician, "who came to us for their practicum experience. We asked them at the beginning of the year to rate themselves on the level of their knowledge about child development and then again at the end of the year. The second rating was significantly lower than the first . . . They became aware of how much they didn't know."

The intimate nature of early intervention services has made interpersonal skills an important concern in professional training. "I think so much time has to be spent on learning a discipline itself," says one therapist. "You are learning how to do certain kinds of things with certain kinds of children. Not enough emphasis is being put on how to work with the parents."

Can you train people to be "sensitive," and to show respect for families, and if so, how? Some feel that effective interpersonal work with parents is not a training issue: you simply have to hire people who already demonstrate this ability. "Having worked with a very large staff," reports one supervisor, "I guess I believe that some people are simply untrainable as far as working with parents." For the majority who feel that such interpersonal skills can at least be influenced, techniques for doing so range from providing good professional role models in practicums to the use of audiovisual feedback. "My greatest influence was a college professor who didn't really teach any particular model at all," says a therapist. "If you involve the parents you will do OK, was her philosophy. It was a very soft sell approach that reached me." "We've found that videotapings of clinical interactions can be very effective," says one training administrator. "But we also have found that if the student can pick the person who will be evaluating a taping they are much more receptive to criticisms."

Continuing education and inservice training are also important tools for maintaining staff quality, although it is increasingly felt to be a financial burden for staff who must pay their own way. "We encourage people on our team to go to outside presentations," says one therapist, "but only if they agree to come back and inservice the rest of the staff about what they learned."

Training for true collaboration between professionals and families will need to take into consideration the family part of the equation as well. An appropriate personnel preparation plan for the new law will also have to address the needs of parents and other family members for training in such areas as communication with professionals, advocacy, and case management.

As goals are established for programs concerning such issues as family support and parental empowerment, it becomes clear that training in a particular discipline alone will not suffice. The question that needs to be addressed in training programs as well as clinical programs is how to promote the interpersonal and interdisciplinary skills that must also be learned. These issues are dealt with further in Chapter 6.

## SUMMARY

The following major statements represent a consensus on current issues in early intervention that will promote quality services when translated into practice:

1. Because of the special timing and intimate nature of early intervention services, family support must be a core service and a primary goal of early intervention services.
2. The goals of early intervention services must include not only those that focus on the developmental status of the child, but also those that promote the child's emotional well-being and foster a supportive and stable family environment.
3. The terminology used to identify practices and goals in early intervention must be carefully and cooperatively defined by service providers and families if communication is to be improved and practices accurately evaluated.
4. Applied methods of scientific observation and improved communication between researchers and practitioners will have an important effect on improving services, and will also provide a framework within which professionals and parents can deal with the uncertainties of their work.
5. The goal of having interdisciplinary, coordinated, family-centered, and community-based services will require important changes in traditional professional and agency concepts of territory.
6. Preservice and inservice training that reflect the already mentioned concerns will be a critical element in bringing the impact of these shifts to bear on services.

Translating these statements into concrete practices may take a substantial reshaping of current attitudes and systems of professional training and service delivery, a difficult and creative process. As these issues are explored, it is important to keep in mind that the motivation for discussing them arises from the growing success of early intervention services and from the recognition of the crucial needs that these services are already addressing. As we look at how services should be improved, and work with the existing but complex requirements of the new legislation, we should also look back on the progress that has already been made.

**"In 1926, my brother with Down syndrome was born,"** says a teacher in an early intervention program. **"He died at 56, when my mother was 87. My mother cried a lot when I was a child. I thought all mothers cried a lot. The isolation was incredible. My mother never in her whole life met or talked with anyone who had a child with Down syndrome. There's a great difference now. I'm telling you about the beginning: there was nothing."**

In the next chapter, we present a summary of some of the major themes that have evolved from the study of early development, and discuss how these themes need to be addressed in designing services for at-risk and disabled children.

# Chapter 2

# Early Development

This chapter will present themes from the study of early child development that are especially relevant to work with at-risk and disabled children, including:

- **the importance of early relationships to development**
- **the transactional and individual nature of development**
- **the use of stimulation**
- **the issue of continuity in behavior**
- **competence in children and families**
- **the interrelatedness of different areas of development**
- **general principles of child development as they apply to the very young at-risk or disabled child**

Included in the findings of Congress in creating Public Law 99-457 was "an urgent and substantial need to enhance the development of handicapped infants and toddlers and to enhance the capacities of families to meet the needs of their infants and toddlers with handicaps." Issues concerning the nature of early child development and its close relationship to family life will play a major role in carrying out this law. It is important that there is a shared understanding of what is known about early development, not just among practitioners but among the various administrative bodies that are involved in implementation of the law. It is a delicate and traditionally private ecology that is being reached by these efforts.

Over the past 25 years, there has been a revolution in our perception of the development of the very young child. The revolution has changed the working image of infancy as a time of passive growth, wherein a parent's competency could be measured in the child's weight gain and absence of diaper rash. We are now looking at early childhood with a microscope that shows us a period of development in which the child's natural endowments interact in complex fashion with the environment, and with caregivers especially, even before birth. Childhood is also coming to be seen as a period in which learning with lifelong implications takes place, and during which parental obligations are spoken of as "helping to foster a competent child." This view of the young child has created a great sense of responsibility in parents and society. From the mother playing Mozart to her child in the womb, to professionals establishing early "school" programs for toddlers, parents and professionals are asking themselves: "What should we be doing for children, and when, in order to aid this complex developmental process"?

For infants born with problems that may interfere with normal development, or for those born with identifiable disabilities, the question takes on a special urgency and seriousness. To what extent can the environment, including professionals and parents, prevent, ameliorate, or compensate for the effects of risk factors or disabling conditions? How much can development be influenced by specially focused early experiences for the child? These are questions that haunt the parents of children with disabilities and the professionals who work with these families. There is an element of mystery about the development of all children, and with at-risk and disabled children, this mystery is even more dramatic.

The long-term benefits of early intervention services, and even some of the constructs that these services are based on, are difficult to study, and results have often been ambiguous or conflicting. But the study of child development has offered a firm general footing for early intervention programs by clearly demonstrating that: 1) important learning occurs at a much earlier age than was once supposed, and 2) the child's environment, including—and especially—the family, provides stronger predictors of eventual outcome than most biological risk factors or disabling conditions. These two well-established principles provide the basic rationale for the family-centered early intervention services that are called for in PL 99-457.

The considered translation of a few basic "learnings" from the area of child development into implications for concrete practices would contribute to improved services. But despite the general acceptance of these principles, they have not been consistently used as guides in the development of services. The purpose of this chapter is to look at themes gathered from the study of child development and to outline the special meaning these themes have for service provision for the at-risk and disabled child. (See bibliographies, categories A and D, for related references.)

## THE EARLY RELATIONSHIP
## BETWEEN PARENTS AND THE YOUNG CHILD

Both research and clinical practice indicate that a key to understanding the development of an individual child is the nature of the child's relationship to parents or other primary caregivers. A responsive relationship between the infant and his or her caregivers is an important positive influence on development. This relationship may be examined in terms of contingent stimulation that fosters learning in the child, or it may be considered using affective terms such as love, but there is general agreement that it has a powerful effect on a child's development.

The infant is known to be an active participant in learning; the infant learns to avoid unpleasant things and to work for those things that bring comfort and pleasure. For the typical child, this learning may occur through our culture's descriptions of proper parenting. For example, the baby cries, and the caregivers respond with cuddling, with a diaper change, or with food. The baby learns that his or her behavior influences what happens and responds by quieting, by smiling, or by cooing, thus letting parents know they have done the right thing.

But with the at-risk or disabled child, these learning scenarios can be radically altered. Premature infants or children with neurological or physical impairment may not have the same sensations of pleasure and discomfort that normal babies do, and they may not be able to respond with the gratifying signs parents understand. In the case of the at-risk and disabled child, the mission of caregiving may first need to be one of careful observation to discover the unique response patterns of an individual child. "One of my really key roles," says a neonatal intensive care unit (NICU) therapist, "is to help the parents have appropriate developmental expectations for their child. I'm thinking of the infant who was born at about 30 weeks and has been in critical care. At 32 or 33 weeks, the infant is no longer in crisis and is growing and healing. The mother comes in with a mobile and a rattle and watches for the baby to respond because now things are going okay. But the baby is just sleeping and the mother needs to know that the baby needs some quiet time, and that in another 2 weeks things may liven up."

*Bonding* and *attachment* are two terms associated with the parent-child relationship. While the terms are often used interchangeably, researchers who are involved in studying these behaviors make careful distinctions between the two. The term *bonding* refers more to the parents', and often specifically the mother's, early feelings for the new child—the bond of affection and responsibility that is usually established. Some researchers stress that the roots of this bond are formed before the child arrives, during the pregnancy itself. It is the bonding of parent to child that is being nurtured by many current trends in obstetrical practices, such as encouraging fathers to play an active role in labor and delivery, promoting rooming-in for the resident mother, as well as various parent education experiences in the hospital.

It is this bonding process that needs special consideration when parents face difficulties either because their child requires extended separation from them, or because they are having problems bonding with a "different" child. "One thing that is sometimes very clear is that parents have a hard time comforting babies who are wired and jittery," comments a pediatrician. "You get into this vicious cycle where the infant is upset and the parents try to pat or jiggle and bounce and do more and more and the parents get more agitated and the baby gets more agitated. We are able to step in and suggest some alternative ways to comfort so the parents can feel close to the baby."

While the early days of the infant's life are important to this bonding process, bonding can occur in different circumstances. Opportunities are needed for the parent and child to be together when both are emotionally ready. It is important for the professional to understand that there are important cultural styles involved in bonding, and the white middle-class picture of bonding is only one of them. "I never know quite how to relate to the issue of bonding," reports a nurse in a large urban hospital. "We work with black American families and Chicano families, we work with Hmong, Vietnamese, Laotian, and Korean immigrants. Each group seems to bond differently. It is hard for me to assess what is good bonding, and what isn't good bonding. I need to be an anthropologist."

*Attachment* refers to the important specific relationship that the child develops with a primary caregiver. Attachment to a caregiver is something that many researchers see as not forming until late in the first year, although the baby is engaged earlier in many kinds of precursory behaviors. Attachment behaviors are dependent on the infant's cognitive development during the first year of life. Some feel that while it is very important for the infant to receive social stimulation early on, this stimulation may be provided adequately by other caregivers when the parents must be separated from the child. In this sense, it may be the *bonding* of parent to child that is more threatened by very early separations than the *attachment* of the child to parents. Both bonding and attachment are clearly critical to the ongoing welfare of the relationship between the child and the parents.

Studies of the parent-child relationship are usually related to the following major questions:

Are differences in early social interaction related to different outcomes in the child's development, either cognitively or socially?

What are the elements of favorable or unfavorable patterns of relationship between parents and children?

Can these relationships be influenced by intervention processes?

While study results have by no means been conclusive, there is a growing body of data to suggest that there is a relationship between early infant-caregiver interaction and later development; this early interaction encourages expanded interactions with the environment and new learning.

What do researchers look for as they approach the study of parent-child interaction? How does one describe attachment or bonding in terms of behavior? Much creative research has been conducted to describe and understand the parent-infant relationship. Some of the behaviors measured include mutual gazing and smiling, parent vocalizations, holding, touching and stroking, and responses to infant behavior such as crying. As these behaviors are carefully evaluated by researchers, questions are refined. What kind of touching is done? How long? With or without vocalization? How does the parent position the baby? Facing? Facing away? Close or distant? How do the parent and child look at each other? For how long? What responses do they offer each other? Researchers have also attempted to relate some of these early observed behaviors to later outcomes in the child. For instance, the child's reaction to the mother's absence at various ages has been measured. Other researchers have attempted to correlate early parent-infant behaviors with later developmental outcomes, such as child performance on cognitive tests at age 2 or even later.

Studies have also explored possible intervention methods when the infant-parent relationship seems to be less than optimal. Various newborn-mother living arrangements in the hospital have been studied to see if there are long-term effects on later mother-child relationships. Other studies have compared parents enrolled in programs designed to explain their premature infant's behavior with parents who were not enrolled in such programs. These studies sought to determine if later measures of both parental adjustment and infant cognitive development and temperament were affected by such programs.

Gradually, as observations and the results of controlled studies accumulate, a picture of the nature of early parent-child relationships is emerging. While there is much ongoing controversy related to this relationship and its role in development, there does seem to be a general consensus on these points:

The parent-child relationship seems to involve more than socially learned interactions between child and caregiver; attachment serves as an influential integrator of experiences for the child, creating a framework on which other kinds of competence may build.

The parent-child relationship evolves with the gradual development of interactional patterns that are unique to each combination of parents and child.

The question is not whether attachment will or will not take place. Some form of attachment seems to take place except in the most disturbed circumstances. It is the quality or type of attachment that is of concern.

The quality of the child's attachment is not determined by the caregiver's behavior alone. The unique characteristics of the infant also help determine the quality of the relationship; the infant's behavior is not a simple, direct product of the parent's efforts.

Attachment is regarded as having an integrative role, as a basic framework for other kinds of learning. Because of this crucial function, the attachment process in at-risk and disabled children becomes of special concern. There is much in the nature of the at-risk and disabled child that can interfere with the development of attachment, to the detriment of the child's already at-risk development. There can be obvious environmental barriers to normal parent-child interactions for at-risk or disabled infants. For example, children may be physically removed from their parents because of health-related problems. Long hospital stays involving the child's dependence on lifesaving equipment may interfere with normal contact between parents and child.

Aside from environmental barriers, the at-risk or disabled child may have physical conditions that interfere with normal social relationships. These may include obvious impairments, such as blindness, or more subtle neurological abnormalities resulting from immaturity or brain damage. "When a child has asymmetric tonic neck reflex," offers a physical therapist, "the mother thinks the child is looking away and avoiding her gaze when she holds him. I try to explain reflex development . . . I think that can do a lot of good for a mother who thinks her child is purposefully looking away. It's not rejection: it's a *reflex*." These kinds of differences may profoundly affect the parents' reactions to the infant, their sense of competence, and their abilities to interact. In this state of personal crisis, individuals can withdraw emotionally from parenting.

While the interaction between premature babies and parents is being studied fairly extensively, studies of attachment in children with disabilities, especially children with severe disabilities, have been more limited. Research shows that attachment behaviors do exist, even in severely disabled children; however, it takes more subtle kinds of observations to identify these behaviors. The signs of attachment tend to be less obvious, less likely to elicit parental response, and not as diverse as in normal children. Studies also suggest that educational efforts designed to sensitize parents to the child's signals can be successful, not only in encouraging the child's interaction, but in influencing the parents' adjustment and coping skills as well.

When a child is born at risk or with an established disability, the *quality* of attachment may be at risk as well. Because of the importance generally placed on this bond in regulating development, helping to overcome the barriers to normal parent-child interactions should be a major goal of early intervention. What kind of relationship is developing between parents and child? If the relationship is going well, would any support encourage its development? If there are problems, what support would help this relationship improve? These questions are important ones to ask in the intensive care nursery, in transitions between service environments, and in the home setting. The questions are also important not just during infancy, but in any work with the very young child. Research has not revealed a cut-off point where attachment becomes unimportant or where it can no longer be influenced.

Even for early intervention professionals who feel that early parent-child interactions are a legitimate focus for their efforts, the directions to take are not always clear. Any effort, however, must begin with careful observation. The study of child development has provided methods of observation that yield subtle information about the behavior of children, even as infants. There are no short cuts to this process of observation, and the *time* involved in observing particular children or parent-child interactions can be a major barrier to this basic step. One way to shorten the professional time required for observation is to help the parents observe well, and such assistance may in itself be a step toward improving parent-child interactions with infants who are at-risk or are disabled. The process of learning how to observe their child can help rebuild the parents' sense of competence, of doing something positive, that is too often lost with the birth of a child with special needs.

There are many creative programs and approaches that attempt to involve parents in observing individual response patterns in their children, and to encourage rewarding interactions between parent and child. These programs are intended to introduce parents to the purposeful behavior of the fragile infant, specifically the subtle signs of alertness and those that say: "I've had too much," or the child's quest for comfort as he or she seeks the protective corner of the isolette. It is apparent to many professionals that helping parents see this infant purposefulness has a powerful effect on their attitude toward the child and toward themselves as parents.

The introduction of services at a time when parents and child are adjusting to each other can help nurture a relationship, but it also carries some risk of coming between the parents and child in unnecessary ways. "One of our major purposes for being here," says a therapist, "is to facilitate the relationship between the baby and the parents. Staff need to be consciously aware of this, because I know I've watched staff doing therapy, and if the child turns to the mother, the teacher will say: 'No, no, now pay attention, don't get distracted,' instead of picking up on that interaction and encouraging it. We need to be much more aware of the subtle ways we may be interfering." "We can," offers another professional, "really alienate the parent and child rather than bringing them together. We can make the parents look at the child as a special-time child and say: 'I have to do these things an hour a day, and if I don't, I'm going to be guilty because I have already produced this defective child and now I'm producing a worse child because I haven't done these things.' With multiple services especially, the parents can become hostages to the professionals they need."

## TRANSACTION

Attachment and bonding are examples of the generally accepted idea that the child's relationship with the environment, including caregivers, is of a transactional nature; the child is influenced by, but also influences, the environment. While the dictionary definitions of *interaction* and *transaction* both involve the meaning of "reciprocal effects between two parties," the term *transaction* began to be used during the 1970s to emphasize the nature of exchanges between the child and the environment. The term *interaction* became associated with a more linear description of development wherein events and circumstances in the environment "interact" with the child to produce certain behavior. The shift to the term *transaction* was made to emphasize that the child's behavior is affected by environmental events, but also that the behavior of the child affects the environment. While the term *transaction* in this context is of fairly recent adoption, it is a description of an easily observable and readily understood phenomenon. "It was not part of my training," offers a developmental pediatrician, "but it is simply a definition of something you knew intuitively could be studied."

Attachment provides a good example of a transactional process. *Interaction,* within the context of attachment, suggests that a mother's behavior, such as lack of emotional involvement because of a child's disability, leads to passivity on the part of the child, a direct linear relationship with the mother as a *cause* of the passivity. *Transaction* considers both parts of the cycle. Children have highly individual patterns of responding: a mother's normal cuddling might actually be annoying to a premature baby, and the baby's withdrawal from the mother's best efforts at nurturance leads to withdrawal on the part of the mother. The term transaction is meant to convey more fully an exchange of influence—that the child is not just a recipient of environmental input but actually helps to determine what that input is.

As a descriptive theme, this use of *transaction* enlightens us not only about the way children learn, but about the way everyone learns from human relationships. We do not merely add material to ourselves as a result of important close relationships; we change, and that change is not one-sided. Teacher and pupil, husband and wife, and certainly parent and child, each becomes different as a result of the exchanges that take place. The early exchanges between infant and caregivers have been observed very closely by researchers. Those particular transactions may instruct the child about what the world is like and how to make one's way in it, because the child's input shapes the behavior of the parent who plays an ongoing role in the child's life.

What special meaning does the concept of transaction—of mutual change—have for the at-risk or disabled child, and what light does it shed on how professionals should guide their practices? At-risk and disabled children can be vulnerable to failure in prompting the environment effectively, and caregivers in the environment may have difficulties in observing, interpreting, and supporting the child's responses. Transactions in these situations may slow down, falter, or break down in ways that are undesirable for both parties.

To prevent this breakdown, we need more subtle observations of the child's behaviors and of the caregiver's interpretation of them. Standard assessment instruments, by their very nature, may focus the professional eye more on what is *not* there than on what *is* there. An assessment instrument may yield an objective score that details a performance deficit, but it may fail to reflect an interactive characteristic that is positive. Standardized instruments may also fail to identify important subtle deficits. "The only screening tool we are allowed to use is the Denver Developmental Screening Test," says one therapist, "but by observation, you can occasionally pick up kids that have problems when their DDST is absolutely normal . . . you can see they have high muscle tone and may have cerebral palsy. I have to do a long narration to talk my way into getting a more complete evaluation for a child like that."

Observation must apply to both parties in a transaction, which means that professionals and parents need to become good observers of their own behaviors as well. "How do you look at people who have not grown up the way you have?" asks a therapist. "One way to learn is to see yourself on videotape interacting with families . . . this is probably the best way to start." Such observations can be of great assistance to parents as well. "I knew a mother who was highly directive with her 2 year old," says a speech-language pathologist. "It was: 'Where's the red block? Give me the red block. Put it there'—very, very directive. We talked with her a lot about this but it didn't seem to be getting through. So, we videotaped a session and had the mom look at it. She understood immediately: 'Oh, so this is what I'm doing.' "

The transactional view of development is ultimately a rather hopeful one, because it turns our eyes to what can be done in the environment to encourage new responses. It should be remembered that the transactional view deals with the domain of experience, or "nurture" rather than "nature." For the child with a disability or even the at-risk child, innate capacities can be seriously limited from the start. The environment and the caregivers are credited with strong influences in the transactional model. There is a danger that failure of the seriously limited child to change will be seen as a failure of the parents, or of professionals, to create the right environment for change. The model should encourage both professionals and parents to focus on the frontiers of the individual child's development as a starting point for possible, though not unlimited, change.

It often falls on the professional to help a parent interpret the dynamic view of development that the transactional model implies. The parent will usually ask questions related to developmental milestones: "Will my child walk and when? Will my child talk and when? What normal things will my child be able to do?" The professional and parent should look together at transactions: What is the child doing now and under what conditions? How can the environment be structured to encourage or discourage existing behavior? "I was having terrible problems with feeding," reports one mother. "Matt's diet was important and I was coaxing and bribing and wheedling and he just kept acting up at every meal. The nutritionist said he was enjoying my efforts and I should try ignoring him. I didn't think much of it, but that night, when he started shrieking, I just ignored him and he stopped, and I gave him a spoonful, and he started shrieking, and I ignored him, and he stopped. Then I finally understood what was going on between us."

## INFANT STIMULATION

"Infant stimulation" was an early expression that became for awhile a synonym for early intervention activities. While the expression is now avoided because of its misuse, "stimulation" does properly describe efforts to promote certain responses and activities in infants and young children. It is known that, from infancy, children have the capacity to respond adaptively to stimulation, to initiate interaction, and to integrate many different kinds of information. There is also an individual but changing tolerance for stimulation in the child, and an associated continuum of adaptive responses to stimulation, from readiness and interest to avoidance and withdrawal.

The terms used to describe infant intervention are familiar to most practitioners, but with casual use many of the terms have lost precision. The term *stimulation* is applied to a variety of early intervention efforts ranging from precise promptings to hanging a mobile over a crib. Stimulation implies the process of exciting the child to activities, growth, or greater activity. Earlier views pictured infants as passive beings who, when shut off from normal experiences as a premature or a disabled baby might be, needed to be aroused or excited or goaded to respond. Stimulation then came to be associated in an undifferentiated way with almost anything that was added to the baby's environment, in the belief that more was better. Continued broad use of the term stimulation can promote the following oversimplifications:

A *certain measured amount of behavioral prompting can result in measurable behavioral output at that moment.* The expectation that an infant stimulation program involving 10 minutes of visual tracking per day will result in an infant who tracks consistently will most likely lead to disappointment. Such expectations fail to consider the role of the infant in such transactions.

*The child depends on the adult to elicit responses.* Again, this idea reflects a "passive recipient" role for the infant and fails to consider the fact that infants learn a great deal without being "taught."

A *"jazzed-up" environment is stimulating for the infant.* From this idea come stimulation efforts that focus on things— rattles, pictures, textured objects, music boxes—without consideration for whether the stimulation is meaningful to the child.

All of these simplifications obscure the importance of transactional processes in shaping the child's behavior.

The critical consideration in efforts to stimulate the at-risk or disabled child is whether the stimulation is meaningful and appropriate for the child. If stimulation is meant to improve the flow of information to the child, it must be done with high regard for the child's capacities, range of perception, and state of alertness at a particular time. To understand how stimulation might be made available requires careful observation.

The determination of what is meaningful and appropriate is not the only concern. One is faced with the question of not only *what* to offer in the way of stimulation but *when* to offer it so it will be most effective. Appropriate timing of stimulation involves the understanding of a particular child's signs of stability and interest, or of the child's need to withdraw. Much has been done to examine the way premature infants signal alertness and readiness to respond. Parents have been encouraged to learn this behavioral language so that their attempts at interactions will occur at times when their child is ready. Many parents of children with disabilities will do this naturally, but the deliberate effort to interpret a child's behavior with help from professionals may make this happen sooner and more easily.

The concerns about infant stimulation programs expressed by some professionals often pertain to the possible fragility of the infant. Should some children and families be left alone for mending and adjusting? Or does the concept of "the earlier the better" take priority? Observations of individual infant behavior and family interactions, rather than reliance on blanket directives or schedules, will point to appropriate decisions. The need for this individual approach is the rationale behind the individualized family service plan in PL 99-457.

## CONTINUITY

The foundation of early intervention services is the premise that development proceeds from global to increasingly differentiated behaviors derived from earlier achievements. This foundation is often referred to as the "developmental model." Recognizing that the exact pattern of this progression is quite individual, one assumes that much of what the child learns as an infant or very young child is important to the development of later competencies: what happens early has a significant impact on what happens later. This premise is basic to the rationale for PL 99-457. Early services are identified as a way to affect such later outcomes as the need for special education and eventual independence.

While this assumption of continuity seems basic to programs that involve doing something early to optimize later outcomes, continuity is a complex issue. Except in the extreme cases, we cannot easily make individual predictions about later development based on biologic risk factors. While many children identified as having cerebral palsy have been found to have had perinatal complications, most children with such complications do not develop cerebral palsy, and many children with cerebral palsy were never labeled "high risk." While the concept of continuity is accepted by many, it is accepted with the idea that the antecedents to any particular developmental outcome are complex, and highly individual, but not reliably traceable. Children may seem to start speaking suddenly, with little apparent preparatory babbling, or may seem to walk without crawling, or match colors without instruction. We usually assume these children have been engaged in preparatory experiences of which we are not aware, or that the elements of continuity did not conform to assumed patterns.

The timing of various kinds of learning has been of great concern to students of child development. There is evidence to support the idea that there are periods of special significance in infancy and early childhood during which there is a particular readiness for certain kinds of learning to occur. At one time, these sensitive periods were referred to as "critical periods." The shift to the term "sensitive periods" has been used to stress the idea that certain kinds of learning may occur more easily, more spontaneously, or at a particular time, rather than to imply that if a skill isn't acquired by a certain time, it will not be acquired at all.

The importance of *continuity* as a premise does not refute the fact that *discontinuities* between early and later development also occur; but, as with continuities, they are not clearly understood. In addition, continuity should not be used to imply evenness in development. The acquisition of one skill can produce sudden and dramatic shifts in transactions between the child and the environment. A child with delayed motor development may, for example, make sudden advances in development in many areas once he or she learns to crawl. The term "continuity" invites simplistic divisions of a person's life experiences into required antecedents to major outcomes, whether positive or negative. In fact, because of the transactional nature of development, the process is never contained in the child alone; the continuity needs to be seen as a continuity of transactions.

Like the concept of transaction, continuity has rather hopeful implications for at-risk and disabled children: it implies that there is a sequence for development that can be discovered and nourished through the right kinds of transactions to move a child forward. However, our impression of the flexibility of child development must always be balanced with a realistic view of the individual child. We are all born with certain innate limitations. For a small percentage of children born with disabilities, the degree of plasticity may be tragically small, and too much hope may be placed in the power of environmental influence.

The concept of continuity is important in the relationship between professionals and children who are at-risk or disabled, and between professionals and families. Evaluation instruments usually rely on the measurement of age-related skills to assess the development of children. This can lead to translating the age-stage descriptive behaviors into guides for what should be done to spur the child's development. If a child can only do two of six age-appropriate tasks on an assessment checklist, the tendency may be to teach the four skills missing so that the child will have a more normal score on the test. Continuity suggests a rather different approach to intervention which focuses more carefully on the child's existing behaviors, identifying new behaviors that might be both within reach and also related to more advanced functional skills. Visual coordination and attention behaviors, for example, are related to many later functional skills, not just to block stacking.

## COMPETENCE IN THE CHILD

The most important lesson that children learn during infancy may be that they can maximize the pleasures of sensation from some simple maneuvers, and can minimize annoyance or discomfort by some others. In short, they learn that they are influential. This sense of being influential is promoted not just by having pleasant things accessible, but by having pleasant things offered contingent on something the child does. In this way, children learn that their efforts make a difference in the world.

The ability of infants to "work" for what they prefer and their patterns of preferences have been well demonstrated: the newborn turning preferentially to the sound of a woman's over a man's voice, or to a nipple with sweetened milk rather than plain milk, for example. The process of mastering tasks has been shown to be an attractive activity as well; the practice and the repetition seem pleasurable in their own right.

The questions that professionals and parents should ask, when normal routes to competence have been blocked because of a disability, seem to be:

What response capacities does the child have?
What are the "good things" to the child?
How can the good things be made available, contingent on responses from the child?

Again, the first priority is observation. Determining the extent of response capabilities in a severely disabled child may require very subtle observations. A child may at first seem to do nothing but cry, or a child may seem to do *literally* nothing.

## PARENTAL COMPETENCE

Competence, a sense of adequacy and control over one's life, is clearly an important goal for parents as well as children. Parents need to believe that what they do counts. The parent who has felt rejected and inadequate because of having a difficult infant needs to learn new ways to interact so the child won't cry so much, or will eat better, or will relax. In addition to learning the skills of observation, the parent may need help in finding the right balance between optimistic challenge to the child's abilities, and acceptance of given disabilities. These kinds of parent needs have been properly respected in PL 99-457. Parent skill-building efforts, which would be described in the IFSP, may be vital to addressing special developmental needs in a particular child. Parental competence is discussed more fully in Chapter 3.

## INTERRELATEDNESS OF DEVELOPMENT

The study of child development has offered an understanding of the interrelatedness of various aspects of development. While it is sometimes important to observe, assess, and encourage motor, cognitive, social, communication, or other features of development separately, these are not discrete areas of competence. Research has shown, for example, the enormous influence that the basic phenomena of attachment has on other aspects of the child's development, as well as the ways that learning and cognition affect relationships and social development.

The implication of this for services to the at-risk or disabled child is that expertise from a variety of disciplines needs to be focused on the child. Children with developmental problems need an *interdisciplinary* approach to assessment and care.

**"Our ability to see what is going on with the child requires our shared perceptions. You have to know there is something to look for or else you don't see it," says an occupational therapist. "I've worked with a speech-language pathologist, a physical therapist, a child development specialist, and a social worker. We all see different things. When we share what we see, it can be very powerful."**

PL 99-457 makes it clear that families are to be full partners on the interdisciplinary team. Parents are in a position to be the model interdisciplinary practitioners, dealing with and observing their children in normal environments and seeing them as complete young family members.

The interdisciplinary sharing of observation leads naturally to better decisions about how goal priorities should be established. "We had a little baby who was doing quite well with gross motor, fine motor, and speech activities. But he wasn't growing at all and he had behavior problems at meals, and the family was really stressed over this. So all of us met together with the parents and agreed to concentrate a month and a half just on the feeding and growth situation. That was what the family really wanted help with, and what the child really needed."

Feeding problems are a good example of the need for interdisciplinary care for the very young child. A feeding problem could signal problems in any or all of these areas: physical growth, nutrition, parent-child interaction, sensory, neuromotor and/or structural characteristics, and stamina. With feeding problems, it is only one possibility among many that the immediate functional problem involves the act of feeding per se. Nutritional factors are certainly a prime consideration when there are feeding concerns about a young child, but they are often intertwined in complex ways with factors such as the parents' stress over the child not eating properly, or over the disruption of family routines. Parents and professionals exploring the physiological and socioemotional factors together will have the best chance of developing a useful picture of the problem.

It should be emphasized that the interdisciplinary approach to the care of children with complex problems is not a new scientific discovery. It is, simply put, knowledgeable people communicating with each other and sharing their strengths as they work toward a common goal. While the concept may be newly refined, the fact that it is sometimes seen as a progressive approach is testimony to how specialized, isolated, and protectionist professional roles have become. The organizational aspects of the interdisciplinary approach is dealt with more fully in Chapter 4.

## PATTERNS OF DEVELOPMENT
## AND THE SPECIAL CHILD

People with disabilities have traditionally been isolated from the mainstream of society. In keeping with that pattern, even professionals who work with children sometimes act as though what they know about patterns of general child development and behavior does not apply to children with disabilities. It is easy to understand why this still occurs. Children with disabilities, especially those with severe disabilities, have behavior that can appear patternless, lawless. They may not respond, learn, or grow in a way that is seen as orderly or predictable. Even the at-risk infant does not always appear to behave in a typical-baby way.

This lawlessness can be disturbing for professionals who do not work with "differentness" on a regular basis. It is not unusual for parents to be refused services, from community pediatricians or dentists, for example, on the basis of the child's disability. "I will take care of your normal children," a physician told one mother, "but I can't take care of this one."

As scientists look closely at the behavior of normal newborns to see how principles of learning and behavior apply to this early age group, they are also learning to look more closely at the sometimes disorderly-appearing development of the special child. We are beginning to see that the at-risk or disabled child is not necessarily operating under a separate set of rules from the normal child; the processes of development described in this chapter apply to the at-risk and disabled child. It is the intervening factors of neurological or physical impairment that make the expression of these processes sometimes appear foreign. The laws may be the same, but they are written in a different behavioral language. Learning to understand the behavioral language of the special child is not a task for the scientist alone. It is a task that can be taken up, with some guidance, by both clinicians and parents who work with at-risk and disabled children. It is the first task of early intervention efforts.

## SUMMARY

This chapter has outlined several of the major points that have emerged from the study of child development, that have particular relevance for at-risk and disabled children, and that suggest ways services should be delivered to them. These are:

1. A secure relationship between the child and a primary caregiver is a critical element in the development of the child's competence and health.
2. The child's relationship with the environment, including caregivers, is of a transactional nature; the child both influences and is influenced by the environment.
3. From infancy, children have the capacity to respond adaptively to stimulation, to initiate interaction, and to integrate many different kinds of information.

4. There is an individual, but changing, tolerance for stimulation in the child, and an associated continuum of adaptive responses to different forms of stimulation that extends from readiness and interest to avoidance and withdrawal.
5. Development proceeds from global to increasingly differentiated behaviors deriving from earlier achievements, but the exact pattern of this progression varies from child to child.
6. Competence develops as the child learns that behaviors are associated with predictable outcomes.
7. All aspects of early development are interrelated. While it is sometimes convenient to look separately at motor, cognitive, social, communication, or other features of development, these are not wholly discrete areas of competence.
8. The above descriptions of child development apply to at-risk and disabled children as well as to normal children. Patience and subtle observation may be needed in order to interpret the behavioral language of the special child, but with guidance these skills can be learned, not only by scientists but also by practitioners and parents.

Without offering specific therapeutic "how tos," we have attempted to suggest the implications that these points have for services. In the following chapters on parent-professional interactions, developmental programs, social attitudes and policies, and organization for service delivery, the relevance of these points to actual practices will be amplified.

# Chapter 3

# Parent-Professional Interactions

This chapter presents themes related to parent-professional interaction in early intervention programs, including:

- the nature of parent-professional relationships
- a redefinition of professional competence
- parent participation in decision making
- parents' early experiences with professionals
- the differing perceptions of parents and professionals
- communication skills
- the factors of time and discontinuity of personnel
- sharing knowledge
- parent-professional matching
- the need for a shared problem-solving model

Strong individual and cultural expectations set the stage for the role of parenting. The preparation of a place in the home—a room, a crib, clothes—is matched by the preparation of a place in the heart and mind that a new child will fill. That place is prepared for a normal child. With few exceptions, the birth of an at-risk or disabled child is not expected. Whether parents stand guard for a few weeks in an intensive care unit with a premature baby, or go through slow months or years of fear as a diagnosis of a disability gradually emerges, their expectations of parenting are frighteningly challenged. For some, a period of medical crises may have as its conclusion a clouded future. Something happens to the parental role of protecting the child from harm. The parents expect to be in control and they are not.

New understandings of early childhood development have made people more likely to question their abilities as parents, as though parenting were now too complex a task for the amateur. Where once a physician was the only regular counsel, parents may now consult with a wide range of specialists, in person or through books, to seek expert help in this task. Early childhood is a time when children and parents develop competence together. The parents learn to be caregivers and a first source of love; the child, through this parental responsiveness, develops the ability to meet and use the world's experiences. While it is now more common for parents in general to look for advice about this process, for parents of at-risk and disabled children, sharing this intimate relationship with professionals is not a matter of choice.

Every parent of a special needs child depends to some degree on help from professionals. The shape and quality of this dependence can influence the ways families adjust and cope with their temporarily or permanently altered lives. While parents with at-risk and disabled children may at times be parents in crisis, they are not often disabled parents. They have capacities for creative problem solving and for coping that professionals must respect, promote, and encourage, while offering their own specialized skills. But professionals can diminish a parent's sense of competence and control that may already be fragile.

The question for early intervention professionals then becomes: How can professionals contribute their expertise and assistance in ways that will respect the family's integrity as well as promote competence and independence in both parents and child? States are clearly directed to answer this question in the new legislation. The individualized family service plan is the driving force behind the effort, and the way this element is articulated will be the states' answer to the question. This plan, to be developed collaboratively by parents and professionals, is to include the following elements:

1. An evaluation of development and skills in the child
2. A statement of the family's strengths and needs related to their support of the child's development
3. A statement of major outcomes for the child and family
4. A statement of services needed
5. Dates of services
6. An identification of a case manager
7. A transition plan when appropriate

As state interagency coordinating councils and lead agencies look at their responsibilities in developing the IFSP, the issues of parent-professional relationships will be played out. The topics outlined in this chapter are ones that we feel will need to be understood and dealt with if the real intent of family support and parent-professional partnerships are to be carried out through this law.

## THE NATURE OF
## PARENT-PROFESSIONAL RELATIONSHIPS

Parent-professional relationships have become a concern largely because of parents who have broken the quiet saint stereotype to articulate their need for services, and their desire not to be disenfranchised recipients of these services. Broad social trends have helped their efforts. The civil rights movement has offered a model. Persons with disabilities and their families were, like other minorities, often not part of making policy decisions that affected them. While some advocacy groups for children and for persons with disabilities have long histories, the consumer advocacy movement that became popular in the late sixties also gave new strength to parental efforts on behalf of children. These trends, along with a growing scientific understanding of the role parents play in the development of the at-risk or disabled child, lend scientific, practical, and moral weight to having parents in charge.

At its best, the parent-professional relationship may never be a relaxed one. While most parents and professionals involved with early intervention services have some experience of productive and warm relationships with each other, complaints are common enough to shape identifiable stereotypes. For the parents, complaints may revolve around professionals who have been insensitive, or who "use" their children for their own education. Parents' greatest concern is that professionals don't value the parents' perceptions of the child's competencies and deficits, of appropriate goals for the child, or of how the child's needs must be balanced with other family needs. For the professionals, the parents can be seen as unrealistic, as making insatiable and exhausting demands for answers, and as people who use professionals as scapegoats for the child's problems or failure to progress.

There are many factors that influence the nature of the relationship between parents and professionals. Like anyone who provides a service, the early intervention professional would like parents to be pleased with, and perhaps even grateful for, their services. But, in the words of one parent: "At the bottom what parents really want is a child who is all right." It is unlikely that the most competent professional will be able to fulfill this wish. "The staff at the clinic is so pleased," says one father. "They have a wheelchair finally adapted for Jim and he's getting around really well. I appreciate their efforts and I want to share in their sense of accomplishment, but what I truthfully feel in my heart is yeah, that's great, but he still can't walk." There may always be that fundamental discrepancy between the parent's and the professional's idea of success.

As professionals deal with parents who are in the early years of caring for a special needs child, they need to keep in mind that grief may be a constant, although sometimes buried, companion for the parents. One therapist reports: "The parents I work with have taught me that they do not go through one grieving period and then reach an acceptance stage. In the first 2 years there are so many milestones that can be a source of renewed grief . . . their child is supposed to crawl, to stand, to say a first word. At first I thought these parents were especially unstable and unaccepting. But I see now that grief is long-term and episodic."

The sometimes adversarial positions of parents and professionals can be a positive part of effective teamwork, in which each party is pushing the other to do their best for the child. But, as with any relationship in which the emotional investment is high, it is easy for both parties to interpret teamwork as "getting someone else to do what I want them to do." Teamwork needs to be seen not as just a means to an end, but as a major goal itself, related to both decision making and to intervention activities. While professionals and parents may share some fundamental goals, there are some inherent differences in their positions. These differences can mask shared objectives and lead to adversarial stances. Teamwork comes about not when these world views become the same, but when each understands something of the other's views, and mutual respect develops from a shared commitment to the welfare of the child. It is this vision that the IFSP is meant to promote.

## REDEFINITION OF COMPETENCE

In working with at-risk and disabled children, the sense of competence felt by both parents and professionals may be threatened. With parents, basic notions of caregiving and protective abilities and of managing a child's development have been altered. In the shock and disorder of having a "different" child, some parents find, at least temporarily, that even their most basic capacities to love are threatened. At-risk and disabled children can threaten professional competence as well. Obstetricians and pediatricians go through their own forms of shock, anger, and adjustment when faced with the birth or diagnosis of a child who is different. Many professionals working in early intervention services have gone through years of education in their respective disciplines. Not only is the practice of their particular skill challenged by the sometimes enormously complex problems of these children, but the parents, with their different needs and priorities, can be seen as barriers to the competent, efficient practice of therapies with the child. It can be the most effective parents, the ones interacting actively with and for their special-needs child, who most threaten the competence of professionals.

---

"It's much easier to take a child into a cubicle for half an hour without the parents," says one therapist, "and then return the child after the session. You don't need to be bothered . . . you can do your thing in isolation. But *easier* isn't the answer. You just aren't going to get much change that way. Real success means involving the parents, too."

---

Parents and early intervention professionals can promote each other's adjustment and sense of competence, but competence first needs to be redefined for both parties. For professionals, disciplinary skills should not be the only measure of competence. However, professional training and administrative policies often work against such an expanded view. As an example, a speech-language pathologist in a rural area includes a 2-year-old child with mild cerebral palsy on her crowded schedule of visits. The young family has been shaken by the diagnosis. The father is withdrawn and embarrassed by the growing differentness of his son and disappears when the therapist arrives. The mother, surrounded by her husband's family, is under constant scrutiny and criticism by well-meaning family members. The busy family farm operation has made support from outside sources, either informal or professional, difficult to find. The visiting speech-language pathologist is, in a sense, the mother's only support system. In the weekly hour that they spend together, the therapist wrestles with two voices: one says her most important goal is to help strengthen and encourage this mother; the other voice pushes her to meet established curriculum goals for encouraging the child's delayed language development. While both goals may develop soundly together, they often do not. Given most program goals and administrative tests of efficacy, if the therapist invests the time to help the mother gain confidence but hasn't gotten through the language agenda, her professionalism may be questioned.

The new legislation definitely supports the integration of these goals through the IFSP, but it will be a difficult shift in orientation for many practitioners and administrators to make. Whether we are talking about general rapport between parent and professional or about specific efforts to involve the parents in a child's therapy, it is probably an artificial distinction to separate the professional's goals for the child from goals for parent-professional interactions. How have the parents been affected by contact with professionals? Are the parents feeling more competent or more dependent, more active or more passive, as a result? The answers to these questions will have a strong influence on the child's environment. The most incontrovertibly positive thing a professional does for a child can be to sincerely acknowledge the hard work and dedication that goes into this special parenting, to say to the parents, simply: "This is not easy—you're doing a good job."

## PARENTS AS DECISION MAKERS

Parent empowerment and parent-professional collaborative decision making have increasingly been a part of early intervention rhetoric. But a concrete understanding of what these concepts mean for professionals is still evolving and may yet lead to revolutionary changes in practices. There are difficult questions to explore. What is the latitude for parent participation in decision making for a seriously ill newborn? For the occupational therapist, the physician, or the speech-language pathologist with years of clinical experience, what does it mean to share decisions with parents who have come to them for help, for relief, or perhaps for a cure?

Despite parent-oriented rhetoric, professionals show mixed feelings about this expanded role for parents. One professional offers the positive view: "For me, parent empowerment means helping the parents acquire some tools or skills for the parenting of an at-risk or disabled child. It means we have to let go of some of our special knowledge to let parents know they can learn what they need to learn." Another case can illustrate the resistance: "We had a case in our program that went to a grand jury for investigation. It was decided there was a definite problem in therapy relationships with parents, and it was also decided that a system needed to be developed between therapists and parents to decide on goals and that type of thing. A task force of therapists from the different units was created to organize the staff training. But it just disintegrated; the task force decided that this was not a real need and they did not want to do it."

A key element in developing appropriate feelings of competence for both the parent and professional is for each to learn when professional expertise is important to decision-making processes, and when the parent is singularly competent to make decisions in the child's best interest. Knowledge is a hard won prize that is sometimes difficult for professionals to pass on. Almost universally, the parents of at-risk and disabled children express, early in their experience, a sense of powerlessness in the face of their child's special condition. A habit of deferring to professionals for everything can easily develop in response to this sense of powerlessness. Such deference can be not only flattering to professionals, but justified in the belief that it is taking some load of decision making from already burdened parents.

On the continuum of decision-making possibilities, there are gray areas where distinctions are not easy to make. A pediatrician plays a critical and legitimate role in making decisions about health related issues. But should the pediatrician tell the mother what bedtime is appropriate, or whether the child should go to a summer play group at the park? Dependence is encouraged when professionals unilaterally make decisions that could more appropriately be made by the parents in the light of individual family styles. This dependence is not compatible with the goal of building a parent's sense of competence. Professionals can help parents take charge by turning the questions back to them: "When does Johnny seem to get tired? When can his father spend time with him? When do your other children go to bed"? It is possible to be helpful in a way that says to parents: "You know what is best."

## FIRST EXPERIENCES

The difficult task of distinguishing between appropriate and inappropriate professional involvement in decisions about the child and family is clearly evident in the medical arena, where most parents will have their introduction to professional care of their child. Parents' first experiences with professionals regarding their special needs child are charged with emotion and can set the stage for evolving attitudes about themselves, the child, and the service system. "I did a home visit with a parent to tell them about the results of a diagnostic evaluation," a social worker reports. "I did a great social work job; it was one of my great cases, and I got the child into a program. I was amazed when I went back 2 weeks later and the parents didn't remember me. You just can't overestimate the trauma parents experience at the time of diagnosis. I've had countless parents say to me: 'All I heard was cerebral palsy,' or 'All I heard was Down syndrome.' "

Because this first contact is often with physicians, the professionals endowed with the highest status, and whose expertise may be the most difficult to share, the stage can be set for dependence. Most early intervention professionals agree that the medical model of diagnosis and treatment is an inadequate model for approaching the chronic problems of children with disabilities. It does not prepare either parents or professionals for the long-term unknowns and unnamed problems that many at-risk and disabled children and their families will face. Nonetheless, remnants of the medical model are still present even in some non-medical community-based settings. The child is diagnosed, the problem is labeled, and interventions are attempted that are meant, if not to cure, at least to result in progress. Goals related to encouraging coping skills and effective problem solving for the child and family are not well articulated by this approach.

The status of physicians in the professional hierarchy of care providers presents its own problems. Despite consumer advocacy in the health care arena and increased demand for accountability, the physician is still a high status person. As a model for other professions, prestige and authority go hand in hand. This stereotype does not lend itself easily to the egalitarian team model that would draw parents into real partnerships with professionals, and both parents and professionals are becoming more aware of this problem. "I gave the neurologist a list of questions I had," said one mother, "including the fact that Angie's muscle tone didn't seem to be anywhere near what it should be. He ran a bunch of tests and then sat down with me and said, 'She has hypotonia, which means she has underdeveloped muscles.' That was it. He got up and left. My pediatrician gave me a copy of the report, and the neurologist really did have a lot to say. He just didn't want to say it to me. Other parents had the same problem with this physician. I won't go to him now; I won't go to someone who won't talk to parents."

Finding the professional balance between promoting competence in families on the one hand, and providing needed expertise and emotional support on the other, is part of a developmental process. A particular kind of support at one time may, at a later time, promote inappropriate dependence. The "syndrome" of the neonatal intensive care unit (NICU) parent provides a vivid example of this developmental process. When a child is born with a life threatening condition, most of the day-to-day care decisions will be made by medical professionals. Sometimes the parents' maximum involvement may be to keep themselves informed about the infant's condition and do whatever visiting is possible. As the child prepares to leave the NICU to go home, the parents experience panic over having to take charge. While the staff was satisfied with the parents' concerned passivity in the NICU, parental dependence may now suddenly be termed "pathological" by staff who are haunted for extended periods of time by parents afraid to make *any* decisions alone.

## Differing Perceptions

Most parents and professionals share the same basic goal of wanting the best possible outcomes for the child. Most often, there are good and caring instincts that lead people into professions involving work with children with disabilities. While glory and financial reward may come to a few, these professions are not generally glamorous in nature. Similarly, most parents of special needs children have good intentions. They struggle to deal with an experience they did not choose; they want, and work hard to provide, the best environment and opportunities for their children. But the steps that professionals and parents take toward shared goals are often not the same kind of steps, and often a sense of trust is missing between the two parties. Both parties may respond to differences with: "Why don't they see things my way"? rather than: "How are they seeing things and why"? For neither the professional nor the parent does life revolve *only* around the child with a disability. Both are influenced by other factors that affect the timing, quality, and intensity of their efforts on behalf of the child.

*One Child Versus Many*   The professional sees many children with disabilities, but the family's focus is centered on one child. The expectations and sense of success with the child are measured therefore with a different eye. This may make professionals more or less optimistic than parents about a particular child's progress. In either case, what is routine for the professional is of vital concern to the parents.

Although professionals are familiar with a vast range of developmentally disabled children, they often focus on one set of rehabilitative and therapeutic goals. When a therapeutic regime is suggested to parents for follow-up in the home, the professional may have unrealistic expectations. One reason is that therapy is not the family's only mission. There are jobs, meals, laundry, other children, and household routines that fill everyone's day, and the family must make time for these responsibilities. If professionals fail to understand this, disappointment and disapproval are sometimes communicated to parents when recommendations aren't followed.

A nurse reports: "I know a child who is at home on kidney dialysis. The doctor was thinking the dialysis procedure was not that big a deal, and he was not listening to the parents. So the parents challenged the doctor to do the exchange, and the doctor found it a very educational experience. Instead of the 20 minutes he expected, it took him 1½ hours to do it. So for the family, doing this every 4–6 hours was a *big* deal. From a clinical standpoint it wasn't complicated, but it was taking over the life of the family."

A therapist relates another example: "Our therapists were trying to work with a mother on toilet training her severely physically disabled little boy. It involved once an hour putting the child on the toilet to sit for 5 minutes. It was fairly strenuous because he was getting heavy and was in braces. We explained the whole system to the mom, showed her the charts to keep. He'd be dry with us all morning and we'd send him home in training pants and he'd come back the next morning in diapers. The mom clearly wasn't following through at all. Finally I took her aside and I said: 'Is something wrong with the toilet training program?' and she just said: 'What's the point? He's never going to do this by himself. I've got three other kids at home; I can't do this every hour.' We just hadn't seen how it fit into her life at that time."

*Socioeconomic and Cultural Bias*  It is difficult to escape the influence of personal biases that may be operating in the relationship between professionals and families of at-risk and disabled children. "We had some training," reports a therapist. "There was this list of characteristics of a family—low income, single parent—and questions about which would be most receptive to your services, and it really made you look at how you judged parents and made assumptions about people before you knew anything about them, based just on labels."

A common bias is that the usually middle-class professionals find the families do not match their ideal environment for a special needs child. For example, single parent households, usually headed by women, are more and more common. Many of these single parent households are part of the growing population of working poor; they are employed women who are living on the edge of poverty. While the professional may be sensitized through training to the stress that the special needs child creates for a family, the stress of poverty may be less well understood. For example, the audiologist is dismayed that a mother doesn't take her daughter to a doctor when the child clearly has an ear infection. Team members shake their heads when, for the third time, an out-of-town family does not appear for their child's scheduled evaluation. A doctor's office visit, transportation costs, meals, and a day away from work all have price tags. Even "free" services may have hidden costs for some families. It is easy for professionals to forget, when the "shoulds" are so obvious to them, that sometimes parents cannot afford to be conscientious.

Socioeconomic status is only one of many labels that can bring out the biases of individual practitioners. "I'm a former military nurse," reports one professional, "and I watch our social workers. When we get a referral from family maintenance services and the dad is a Marine, immediately, there's this stereotype of authoritarianism: the fathers have sergeants cracking down on them so they are going to turn around and crack down on their kids."

*"Problem" Families* Frustration with a family's home environment is certainly not always the result of unsympathetic, middle-class professional bias. Most professionals will have contact with some families for whom the problems associated with a special needs child are among many seriously debilitating factors in the life of the family. For the teacher or therapist focusing on the developmental needs of the child, these extreme and complex family problems can be the source of terrible frustration and sadness. "I can deal with poverty," offers a nurse. "I just can't deal with poverty with people who don't speak my language and who can't get welfare, food stamps, or clothing because they are illegal immigrants."

Families can have combinations of chronic problems that might include unemployment, poor nutrition, inadequate housing, chronic illness in family members, and depression or other emotional disorders. Additionally, there may be social isolation, substance abuse, the absence of any routine in the home, and physical or sexual abuse among family members, including abuse of the special needs child. The special challenges presented by these multiple factors can be overwhelming even with multiple agency involvement. Professional reactions may range from a sympathetic understanding of the complex problems faced by the family with a special needs child, to exasperation over the family's inability to "get it together." This range of reactions can also exist *within* an individual professional at different times. Early intervention professionals in these settings need their own forms of support if they are to set appropriate goals for their efforts and also maintain respect and empathy for the families.

There are existing programs that deal directly and openly with the issue of "problem parents" and that make support for such parents a priority. Many of these programs focus on teenage single mothers as a group at risk for becoming dysfunctional parents. The goals for these programs sometimes do not even refer directly to the children. One social worker reports: "Many of these mothers are withdrawn and quiet. They have no confidence in their mothering skills. They have all the uncertainties of other teenagers, and the responsibilities of not only a baby but a disabled one, to take on. We work on some basic things that have to do with making them feel better about themselves, convincing them that they, too, can become good mothers and encouraging them to make use of their support systems—often their mothers—so they can spend some time still being a teenager without feeling guilty." PL 99-457 offers new hope for early interventionists working in these difficult situations, because it makes clear the connection between the family and the child's developmental needs.

*Diagnostic and Assessment Views*   Parents and professionals often have a difficult time communicating about the state of development and the accomplishments of individual children. Again, this can be a result not of error on either side, but of different definitions and views of these accomplishments. Professionals, for the most part, are operating under standards of evaluation that may be rigid. A child is said to be walking, on a particular behavior checklist, when he or she can walk across a room unaided. Most parents will say their baby is walking when the child takes the first few steps and plops down amidst adult applause. Parents of special needs children, like most parents, give their child credit for beginning skills. At an evaluation meeting, the parents say Johnny is walking. The physical therapist disagrees, and jots down a note about excessive optimism on the part of the parents. The parents come away feeling misunderstood and humiliated by their own enthusiasm. Often, the difference in definitions is not acknowledged.

An additional problem is the use of undefined or vague terms. Such terms can often leave parents and professionals with quite different understandings about what has actually been communicated. One parent reports:

> **"When they said 'delayed' I thought of all the trains going from New Jersey to New York. Jeff's on a slower train, but he's going to get to New York. They knew all along he was never going to get to New York. Their 'delay' was my 'off the track.' "**

Another major source of frustration and anger for parents is the lack of agreement among various professionals. This is not always due to differing levels of professional expertise. For example, it is difficult to predict with accuracy the level of function in very young at-risk or disabled children. Another source of frustration comes from personal and sometimes group professional attitudes toward at-risk children. There is research evidence showing that not only do individuals have their own patterns of positive or negative outlook, but there are also predictable biases along professional lines. Studies have shown that pediatricians, for example, have a more pessimistic view of the ultimate level of function for a moderately mentally retarded individual than do psychiatrists or speech-language pathologists. Other biases relate to realms of responsibility. The neonatologist releasing a stabilized infant after months of medical crises may see the child's status very positively because certain medical goals have been achieved. A therapist may soon after communicate serious concerns to the previously relieved parents. To demand a consensus may at times be unrealistic, but parents need help in integrating the various views.

*Focus on Problems* Professionals may focus only on what can be done about the things that are "wrong" with a child or a family. Visits to such professionals can be depressing ones for parents when, even though their child may have made happy progress, the professional eye remains on deficits. The parents, too, may come to think of their child as a bundle of problems or a case. "I have found it really helpful to start out saying something nice," says one practitioner. "To say something positive like: 'Look how well your baby grabs my hand.' I had one mother burst into tears because I was the first person who ever said anything positive about her baby." PL 99-457 has attempted to address this issue by requiring an assessment of family and child *strengths* as well as needs. It will not be an easy focus to redirect, however.

## Communication Skills

Communication is the key to improved parent-professional interactions. The professional who is sensitive and respectful of parents will communicate not only warmth and empathy but will also effectively communicate information about the child. Gaining knowledge and understanding is one way parents become independent, competent caregivers for their children. Some professionals tend to hold information back, not because they wish to consciously retain control, but because they feel they will be opening the door to inappropriate involvement of the parent or to unnecessary worries and fears.

A common complaint of parents is that communication is not even directed toward them, but rather toward other professionals or trainees interested in the case their child presents.

**"It happens so easily when we bring our residents in for genetic counseling clinics," reports one pediatrician. "They get so carried away diagnosing the case, they discuss genetic malformations back and forth with each other, without considering the parent or the child who is sitting there quietly listening. The discussion and the training of the resident should not take place at the expense of the parents and children."**

It is often tempting for the professional to adopt the role of the knowledgeable decision maker and to encourage the parent to adopt the role of the passive recipient. Both parents and professionals need to go through the sometimes painful process of altering these roles if the goal of effective partnership is to be achieved. Communication between parents and professionals is frequently set in the style of a medical briefing. Although it is acknowledged outwardly that the parent knows the most about the child, in practice it is still the professional, by virtue of years of specialized training, who assumes the role of information giver. Team meetings are not organized often enough around the premise that the parent has important observations to share that can help the professionals in their tasks. One therapist comments: "For a while we were dealing with parents who were not informed and we had to spend a great deal of our time teaching vocabulary. Now, more and more, the parents are teaching us. They sometimes have the time and the drive to keep up with things that we don't know about. They come in talking like doctors and actually know more about their child's syndrome than I do. It's definitely possible to share information and develop real partnerships, but it requires effort on both sides."

More balanced communication between parents and professionals is a well-accepted goal, but the path to it is not well defined. Preservice training is certainly one place to start. Medical schools, responding to growing criticism about the lack of interpersonal sensitivity among their graduates, are beginning to include classes on interviewing and communication skills in their curriculums. But planners of training programs, in medicine and elsewhere, must meet the demand to expose students to a constantly growing body of technical knowledge, while at the same time trying to make a place for more humanistic and interactional concerns in the curriculum.

There is no short cut to improved communications skills, and formal training is not always the answer. Some programs attempt a more experiential sensitization to communication, in which students are assigned long-term follow-up or informal contact with families, allowing the use of newly acquired technical skills to be put in the context of overall human needs. The experiential approach is based on the idea that good professional role models and the right family experiences are the best training tools.

Training for parents needs to be part of the process as well, and should be seriously considered as part of personnel development plans. Training in ways of communicating effectively with professionals and of obtaining at meetings the information they need is one important area. Advocacy and case management are also areas for parent training that can contribute to collaboration skills.

## Time and Discontinuity of Personnel

Lack of time and discontinuity of personnel are two major barriers to effective parent-professional collaboration. These barriers are especially notable and difficult to break through in the medical setting. The parent may establish comfortable communication with one neonatologist, only to find she is replaced in a few weeks with another house officer who is not only distant, but who also offers a different prognosis to the parents. The negative effects of discontinuity can be alleviated to some extent if there is a case management system in place. Attempts have been made in some programs, for example, to have a social worker from the intensive care unit take part in the later follow-up conferences in the pediatric clinic. The IFSP in PL 99-457 calls for a case manager from "the discipline most relevant to the infant's and toddler's or family's needs" as well as for a transition plan.

Many parents find that the time they spend with professionals, especially at the time of diagnosis, is inadequate. Although efforts are being made to improve this situation, horror stories of parents learning of their child's serious disability in a 10-minute consultation are not rare. "We have to work hard to create adequate time," says one administrator. "We have medical therapy conferences that the parents attend. The physicians who do these conferences with us usually also do other clinics in the hospital, and they will constantly complain: 'We could double what you are bringing through, let's speed it up a little.' But one of our credos is that if the family needs the time, they get it, and the other staff will not let the physicians leave. We rig it so they don't have any choice."

## Sharing Knowledge

Sharing professional knowledge with parents in an understandable form is a critical element in building parental competence and in developing parent-professional collaboration. This includes sharing information about other professionals or programs as well as knowledge about the disability itself.

Professionals need, among other things, to learn the appropriate use of the words: "I don't know." Parents want information about their child's future that the professional may have only limited ability to provide. Out of professional and personal pride, and out of a desire to offer parents what they so desperately want, professionals may share thoughts about the near or distant future functioning of a child. These predictions may later prove either too pessimistic or too optimistic, and may add to the parents' distrust. A shared understanding of the limits of prediction is needed, balanced with the professional's obligation to communicate those "knowns" that are critical to the parents' planning and adjustment.

## Parent-Professional Communication and the Use of Jargon

There has been much talk about the use of jargon by professionals. Every profession develops a vocabulary that facilitates communication with like professionals or that makes communication more precise. There is a distinction between technical language that facilitates communication and jargon that substitutes high-tech words for perfectly adequate lay terms. One way to help ensure that knowledge about a particular child is shared effectively is to make sure that parents leave a conference with written information to back up an explanation of a diagnosis or therapeutic procedure. Parents may react emotionally during a conference, and later find their recall is sketchy. Later, these parents must often serve as experts on their child's condition for family and friends. Written materials help them, for example, to answer a grandmother's questions or to ward off a neighbor's well-intentioned but inappropriate advice.

Professionals in any specific area need to pass on information about other resources for parents and children. When parents have to ferret out available services completely on their own, it makes them angry and suspicious of their professional contacts. Sometimes this suspicion is well founded. The element of "turf" protection does exist. It can make professionals reluctant to send families to other professionals who may contradict their own recommendations or who may interfere with a program that is conveniently in place. But more often, it is a case of unintentional professional isolation and lack of information. A pediatrician should know about community early intervention programs available for a toddler with Down syndrome. Similarly, the therapist involved in home visits should know about respite care programs for an exhausted mother. The central directory of resources that states must have as part of PL 99-457 should greatly help in meeting this need.

Parent-to-parent support is a key resource for professionals to share with parents. When such support is not established locally, professionals can get involved in helping parents get started. This support can offer powerful therapy for parents.

While many professionals have been uneasy about groups that might encourage "troublemakers," parent-to-parent support has been not only an important source of emotional support for the parents, but has also encouraged understanding of professional viewpoints and of effective ways of working with professionals.

## Matching

It is clear from parents' reports and the reports of professionals that whatever mechanics and rules are established to improve communication between parents and professionals, the bottom line involves individual personalities. There are parents who will be "problems" even for the most sensitive and patient professional. There are professionals who will be "problems" too, acting cold and unresponsive no matter how much sensitivity training they have had. More experiences with families for professionals, and more training for parents may help ease these situations, but the problem of difficult personality styles will never be eliminated.

We have stressed in this chapter the intimate nature of professional involvement with the parents of the very young child, and the way this involvement can affect the timing and ultimate adjustment of parents and families. For this reason, there is a process of matching that ideally should occur between families and professionals. There are some professionals who can work well in partnership with families who are confident and aggressive in the demands they make. This same professional may not be the right kind of person to draw out the family that is passively absorbing the blows of their new responsibilities. While this matching may not be possible in some settings, flexible case management can make it a reality in other team situations.

When parents talk about their contacts with professionals, there is usually at least one person who was a special match for them and whose contact extended into an alliance that was very much like friendship. Among inarticulate, shy, or intimidated parents, those who, for whatever reason, feel they cannot influence, this experience will be less likely to occur. With professionals whose workdays are filled with contacts with families and children and with the demands of paperwork, parents who don't make themselves known may not get the attention they need. If parents and professionals truly work collaboratively on the IFSP, and on the identification of an appropriate case manager, appropriate matches should be more common.

## Shared Problem Solving

Finding the correct diagnosis through a maze of symptoms is a critical need for parents. They want to know what it is their child has. They need to know the etiology of a child's disorder. But even when these questions can be answered definitely, which is often not the case, professionals need to focus themselves and the family on practicalities. Parents and professionals need to be drawn into a problem-solving diagnostic process that leads to the question: "What should we be doing?" rather than: "What should we call it?" This process should not focus just on problems related to the child's development, but on the family situation as a whole. What, in the child's special status, is most straining family resources? How should goal priorities be set? A therapist can understand a family's lack of interest in developmental activities when he or she knows the parents are spending 6 hours a day feeding their child.

Parents may often withdraw, after an initial period of interest, from participation in various aspects of early intervention (e.g., meetings, play groups) because they find they do not understand their purpose. They may feel that they are only learning new names for the things they are observing themselves, sometimes more accurately, at home. Problem-solving relationships are important for families wishing to make contacts with professionals meaningful and useful. The opposite side of the problem, when parents insist on visits for which the professional can see no function, also occurs. Parents also need to learn what efforts are productive with their child, or when maturation is needed before new efforts are attempted. (See bibliographies, category G, for references by parent authors.)

# SUMMARY

In this chapter we focus on the transactions between parents and professionals and their importance in early intervention efforts. Major statements include the following:

1. While parents with at-risk and disabled children may at times be parents in crisis, they are not disabled parents. They have capacities for creative problem solving and coping that professionals need to respect, promote, and encourage.

2. Parents and involved professionals may have widely differing perspectives, experiences, and goals for a particular at-risk or disabled child. The difficult process of sharing and of learning to understand these differing perspectives is an important part of care for the child.

3. To foster independence and competence in families, and to make the most effective use of services, it is critical for both parents and professionals to distinguish between times when professional participation is important for good decisions, and times when the parent is singularly competent to make decisions in the child's and family's best interest. Inappropriate dependence is encouraged when professionals make decisions that should be made by parents.

4. Finding the professional balance between promoting competence and independence in families, on the one hand, and providing needed expertise and emotional support on the other, is part of a developmental process. A particular kind of support at one time may, at a later time, promote inappropriate dependence.

5. The goals of a partnership and teamwork between parents and professionals are difficult ones. The easiest pattern is for the professional to adopt the traditional role of knowledgeable decision maker and the parents to adopt that of passive recipients. Changing these roles takes commitment by both parties.

6. Lack of time and discontinuity of personnel are powerful barriers to effective parent-professional collaboration.

7. The professional needs to share large amounts of information, often of a technical nature, with the parents of special needs children. This process can be aided by appropriate translation of technical language, the provision of relevant written materials, open acknowledgment of unknowns, and direction to other service resources.

8. Professional collaboration with families who have very young special needs children has a strong interpersonal component. Case management should allow professionals who develop a rapport with a particular family to take more responsibility for working with that family, and should also ensure that every family has an advocate.

9. Parents and professionals need to be drawn into a problem-solving diagnostic process that leads to answers for questions such as: "What should be done?" and "What should it be called?"

10. Articulate, active parents have brought the issues of parent decision making into the spotlight, but not many start their careers as "special needs" parents with the skills to make it happen. It is part of the professionals' job to help parents identify goals and develop resources within themselves and within the service community to achieve them.

In the following chapter, we focus on issues concerning early developmental services for children, building on themes related to both early child development and parental-professional collaboration already outlined in previous chapters.

# Chapter 4

# Developmental Programs

This chapter considers the following issues related to programs that promote the development of children at risk or with disabilities:

- the "curriculum" approach
- the assessment-intervention continuum
- qualitative versus quantitative measures of efficacy
- interdisciplinary function and the inter-relatedness of development
- the balance of usual and special needs in care planning
- goals for developmental programs
- parent-professional collaboration

A ttempts to influence early child development, commonly known as "early intervention" programs, have been justified from a number of perspectives, from the cost effectiveness of having at-risk and disabled children eventually become more productive and independent citizens, to the goal of improved quality of life for the child and family. While PL 99-457 emphatically broadens family concerns, the issue of child development is still at its core.

Even when a newborn is in medical crisis, long-term developmental concerns surface. Parents want to know if their child will develop normally, and if not, how abnormally: Will she talk, or walk? Will she have learning problems in school? Professionals share this concern as they try to map out a constructive course of action for the family. For both parents and professionals, the critical question is: "What should we be doing, and when, to aid the developmental processes of the child?"

## THE "CURRICULUM" APPROACH

Core questions for developmental programs include: What are the child's immediate and long-term developmental needs? What, from our knowledge of child development and our experiences with parent-professional interactions, should be considered in planning the content of an intervention program? Programming is one area wherein the gap between what is known about child development and what is practiced in services is most apparent. There are probably many reasons for this, but a major one is that what is known suggests program practices that are often more difficult and more time consuming than what is conventionally funded and practiced. (See bibliographies, category E, for related references.)

It is known that the young child is engaged in important learning very early in life. But what we are finding out about infant responsiveness often has been naively translated into ideas about "teaching" skills in a "curriculum." For example, as infants were found to attend differently to regular versus scrambled human facial masks, efforts were made to "teach" children to look at themselves in a mirror, or "teach" them to look at hand mitts with facial features, as part of an organized curriculum. The most simplistic application of the term curriculum is the use of standard "how tos."

The term *curriculum* is so tied to traditional concepts of teaching and instruction that it conveys a "take-charge" attitude, leading to statements such as: "We need to *intervene* early with at-risk and disabled children so we can *train* parents to *teach* and stimulate their children." But a new vocabulary is gradually softening these meanings. We now speak, for example, about partnerships and joint efforts of professionals and parents, about the individual needs of children and families, and about care, support, nurturance, assurance, and guidance. In addition to a continuing concern with content and specific procedures, there is more emphasis now on the flexible processes of assessment and intervention. Observation, interpretation, listening, and sharing between professionals and parents is emphasized more.

This new language reflects an important but not always convenient shift in emphasis. But new words alone are not enough to counteract the tendency for professionals to develop set ways of approaching the care of the child. "We have a good teacher training program," says one administrator, "and we are focusing on interaction and on training our teachers to work on functional kinds of behaviors rather than on behaviors in a strict sequence. Interestingly, we've had to fight to keep the 'functional' model from becoming rigid, too. Functional skills are also sequenced because it's a data-based program and we've got to collect data. We still aren't really focusing on the interactions that are going on. It was a good idea that kind of soured on us."

It is not professionals alone who lean toward a "curricular" approach to developmental efforts. "When Andy was first born," says one father, "I read a book on teaching Down syndrome infants with all these charts and sequencing and I really got into it at first. But you have to use common sense. I mean, it says you have to do this 20 times before you go on to the next thing, and Andy is never going to do something 20 times the right way."

The more rigid curricular approach has become a liability to appropriate developmental assessment and intervention with at-risk and disabled young children. As early intervention services were developed, it became common for programs to be based on a "developmental model." Programs took on respectability as the assessments and curriculums became more standardized and therefore easier to evaluate and improve. This has encouraged a more disciplined and systematic approach to child development. But wider use has also led to a rigidity that has not kept pace with new understandings about child development. Transactional phenomena influence how and when families and children achieve developmental competence and, in part, account for individual variations in rate, pattern, and style of change and development. Scales and checklists based on sequential stages describe the progression of developmental characteristics. They do not take into account both child and family status in a way that realistically reflects the child's strengths or the barriers that affect child development.

A serious liability of the concentration on standardized tests and checklists is that relatively unimportant behaviors can become the entire focus of a child's intervention program. Primary and secondary school programs have been criticized for content that aims only at having children score well on school achievement tests. Professionals working with very young at-risk and disabled children can also unwittingly concentrate on behaviors such as "reaching toward mirror image," that will raise the child's developmental test score but that may be irrelevant to current functional needs or to the child's interaction with people. Furthermore, a test item may be both nonfunctional and currently unachievable. Attempts to teach block stacking or the manipulation of certain toys before the child can sit will be met with frustration and failure. Such tasks become useful only when they are consistent with the child's developmental readiness and are related to more complex functional tasks.

However, aside from the security that professionals and parents may feel in following a developmental checklist and prescribed observations, there are also administrative pressures to keep a more rigid developmental approach in mind. "I'm still struggling a lot in terms of keeping the data that's asked of me by my agency," says one therapist. "We're so into this 'roll the ball 10 times' type of thing. I think society has forced therapists and teachers to forget about things like interactions between the child and parents. You can say this child is interacting 50 times with the parents, and the insurance companies are going to say: 'Well, big deal,' and the legislators are going to say: 'Well, big deal.' You need money, so you say that because of this program the child has gone from a 6-month developmental level to 12 months and they say: 'Hey, you've got your money.' " Basic data collection requirements in early intervention services are required of states under the law. In addition, federal efforts will be made to evaluate the effectiveness of programs in cooperation with the states. It will be important to resist convenient but over-simplified evaluations that are not consistent with the important mission of the law.

## ASSESSMENT-INTERVENTION CONTINUUM

Many people have recognized the limitations of a curricular ap-proach to intervention, one based on a strict reference to de-velopmental norms or even a strict reference to functional skills. "But it's very hard to get away from a developmental curricu-lum," says one therapist. "It's hard to know how to move on; we know what is wrong but we haven't found the alternative we need."

Viewing programming for the child as part of an assess-ment-intervention continuum enables professionals to use cur-ricular approaches in a flexible, scientific, and creative manner. The concept of an assessment-intervention continuum suggests that assessment should not be a discrete activity of a child's pro-gram, followed by equally discrete activities labeled as interven-tions. A creative function of assessment is not just to obtain a developmental score for a child, but also to identify what par-ticular competencies are logical starting points for program ac-tivities. Observations by the team and the parents during an assessment can complement objective test results and lead natu-rally into more effective intervention efforts. Likewise, observa-tion during particular intervention sessions provides an ongoing indication of what works without a formal reevaluation.

"My assessments would not be very valid if I stuck only to the formal procedure," comments a therapist. "One father said to me: 'I don't know why he wouldn't put pegs in that board today . . . at home he goes to the drawers and gets this thing and sticks it right into his high chair, just like what you were trying to get him to do today.' This tells me not only that the child has the skill, but also points right away to some other ways to approach his program." An assessment that can be used to provide some indication of intervention needs and goals is not just an assessment of the child's status, but also an assessment of what kinds of strategies seem to work best with the child. A therapist was trying to get a child to imitate "mama" during an assessment. No amount of urging for eye contact and vocalization was successful. An observer noted that the child *was* responding in other ways. When the therapist could identify times when the child, on his own, looked to the adult to smile, vocalize, and play, these interactions could be used to advantage. An oversimplified approach to quantifying and itemizing behaviors required for developmental checklists may not foster such flexibility.

Using assessment strategies and techniques as the bases for ongoing developmental care is also important when considering the care of infants in the NICU. During assessment, team members' impressions about interacting successfully with the baby can yield valuable information about the child's maturity, physiological stability, and attending behaviors. Such information is important for continuing successful caregiver-infant transactions beyond the assessment process.

Assessment as intervention is an idea that is gaining some credibility. It places the emphasis not solely on a child's quantitative test score but also on the need to know more about the child's reactions, strengths, and deficits in interactional style. It also emphasizes how the parents interact with the child and how to mobilize resources of people and things on behalf of the child. This approach also constructively leads away from intervention that uses a checklist to set goals for teaching "missing" skills.

Assessment should be considered as a process of observation rather than as specific procedures done with the child. The individual complexities of the child's behavior can then guide the selection of useful assessment instruments.

An assessment that points to intervention processes identifies whether learning is being generalized from the assessment situation to interactions with parents and other family members or caregivers. A psychologist providing services with a young, physically disabled child was gratified when the child began making simple choices among materials and activities in structured learning situations. Later, observing the child with his parents and sibling, the psychologist saw that family members played with the child without the child making decisions about whether he wanted a story or his truck, a record or the toy horse. Clearly, the child's progress in the structured program represents limited success (none, really) if his daily activities and family interactions are not positively influenced. Too often, developmental intervention is seen as occurring in scheduled contacts with professionals. This approach will be reinforced if IFSP goals specify things such as: "Child will reach for ball, in ten trials, by December 1." Such goals traditionally have been met by crediting isolated, fragmented responses without consideration of meaningful generalization of skills.

## QUALITY VS. QUANTITY

Numerical and quantitative measures can be efficient indices of a child's developmental status, and *can* serve the assessment-intervention continuum process. The emphasis needs to be more balanced, despite the added time and observation skills needed, between appropriate quantitative recordings of behavior and qualitative ones. For example, an important developmental characteristic of a child's vocal behavior during the first year of life is the reciprocal nature of vocal exchanges before true words are used. The importance of nurturing such an aspect of development can be lost when the emphasis is on the frequency with which a child vocalizes in a structured situation. It is not uncommon for a clinician to encounter two children with the same quantitative score on a test. Most clinicians recognize that this does not mean that the program efforts that work with one will work for the other as well. Focusing only on the quantitative aspects, the presence or absence of a skill, in assessment processes will also fail to point to emerging skills or behaviors leading up to "goal behaviors."

The quantitative description of behaviors has other drawbacks. It takes experience and subtle observation skills to understand what is going on in terms of adaptive development with an at-risk or disabled child; the form of this development may be unique to the child's particular disability. Deaf children often develop their own compensatory communication modes that are unstandardized but lawful. Current measures of child assessment do not necessarily direct us to these kinds of observations, because the adaptation is generally not amenable to standardization. Quantitative measurement is clearly needed, but to obtain the most useful information, we must first improve measurement strategies and instruments for use in process-oriented planning and care. Efforts to measure adaptive skills from the point of view of measurement strategies as well as measurement instruments are a current focus of attention. (See bibliographies, category E, for related references.)

## INTERDISCIPLINARY FUNCTION AND THE INTERRELATEDNESS OF DEVELOPMENT

In the chapter on early development, it was stressed that certain laws or patterns of child development apply to at-risk and disabled children as well as to normal children. Recognizing the particular expression of that lawful behavior in the special child requires careful observations on the part of parents and professionals. Effective programs that continually assess needs and look for creative ways to meet them are tied to this same process of careful observation. Things such as curriculum guides, developmental checklists, and materials must serve this process, not determine what it is. To bring the definition of curriculum in line with this idea, it must include reference to both the *content* and the *process* of a program. Curriculum in early intervention has been productively defined as the planned interaction of children and families with time, staff, and materials.

Another important offering from the study of infant development with implications for the content and process of curriculum is that the various aspects of development are interrelated. With the very young child, the distinctions between socioemotional, cognitive, communication, and sensorimotor development are particularly difficult to consider or influence separately. The child with sensorimotor dysfunction may not have the visual-motor control or the exploratory abilities that are important avenues for cognitive development. The child with communication dysfunction may not be able to draw people into the interactions important to social development. The convenience of speaking about and studying these different aspects of development as separate entities, however, has obscured the interrelatedness of developmental areas.

Concern for this interrelatedness should not be interpreted as a diminished need for skillful disciplinary assessment and care. The value of an interdisciplinary approach lies in the combined disciplinary expertise that allows close scrutiny of various aspects of development. This information is then available for interdisciplinary interpretation, synthesis, planning, and practices that will promote the infant's integrated development along multiple lines. Such interdisciplinary function is contrasted with separate disciplinary planning and goal-setting, which leaves the parents struggling to integrate the various strategies designed to promote their child's overall development.

Because of the complex nature of problems for at-risk and disabled children and the interrelatedness of various developmental concerns, decisions about what should be done for a child and who should be in charge of doing it should result from interdisciplinary decision making. PL 99-457 takes this need into account by calling for the IFSP to be developed by a team made up of the family and professionals from multiple disciplines. Interdisciplinary decisions are more than the *sum* of thinking of professionals and parents; shared perspectives lead to more accurate observations and evaluations, and more appropriate and thoughtful recommendations.

While the rationale behind interdisciplinary decision making is obvious, it is in fact a difficult process, one that requires an understanding of group process and of decision-making techniques. It also takes hard work, practice, and trust. Making decisions using an authoritarian model is an easier process than making decisions through a consensus building model. "It's difficult at a personal level, I think," says a speech-language pathologist. "You risk a great deal. I put out something I'm doing and I risk having someone else look at it and say it's not the right approach. We risk having to take the time to work out what the priorities are. I may not be able to put my speech and language first with a particular child. The more I work with other people, the more I have to give up my narrow trajectory, and sometimes that's very difficult for me." In addition, professionals come to the process with a legacy of unequal professional status and with professional biases. Parents come with a legacy of not being considered part of the team and of feeling the professionals are the knowledgeable ones. All contribute individual personalities that may be more or less amenable to the give and take required for team interaction.

Different teams interpret interdisciplinary function in different ways. *Transdisciplinary* team interaction may be a special case of interdisciplinary function in which team members cross disciplinary boundaries, teaching and learning across disciplines. The team authorizes one person to be involved directly with the child and family, rather than with a whole team. With a child who has a feeding problem, for example, an occupational therapist might be involved in helping the child and parent develop better interactions, implement feeding routines, and improve handling and positioning, but the program would be created and monitored by the entire transdisciplinary team.

There is some controversy over the extent to which one discipline can take over for another. "My difficulty is this," says one therapist, "I think for some kids you can have one person pretty much do a whole program, but I think there are other kids who really need the expertise of the person who is trained in that discipline." "Evaluation and reevaluation are two functions I would not delegate to someone outside a discipline," says an administrator. "I don't have a background in physical therapy," offers a teacher, "but on the other hand, nothing more is being asked, at least not much more, than is being asked of the parents. If the parents are supposed to be able to do the therapy, I should be able to do this, too."

The transdisciplinary approach may *appear* to have fiscal appeal when it is inaccurately interpreted as cutting down on staffing requirements. Appropriately carried out, it does not require fewer staff. Implementation of the transdisciplinary approach requires more qualified individuals in order to authorize one or a few persons for direct interaction with families. In understaffed and underfunded programs, it may fall on a lone therapist to provide services without effective participation by other disciplines in decision making. Such programs may feature the crossing of disciplinary boundaries, but only by default. Crossing of boundaries by default is inconsistent with, and inimical to, the transdisciplinary approach.

Ideally, the IFSP should relieve families of having to put together an interdisciplinary consensus from separate consultations with professionals, a responsibility that in the past often fell to them. Instead, the family and the professionals together arrive at a consensus regarding IFSP outcomes. The quality of this process, however, can be no better than the quality of the disciplinary expertise, mutual respect, and group skills of participants.

## THE BALANCE OF USUAL AND SPECIAL CARE NEEDS

A first step in any program is to identify the range of needs that the at-risk individual or disabled child may have, and to determine which, if any, of these needs correspond with the services of the particular program. The broad areas of need to be identified are: *health care, developmental,* and *family* needs. Just as the various features of development are closely associated, these areas of need are interrelated as well. It is impossible to consider an effective developmental program for an infant without regard for the child's health status and family environment. In each of these three areas, there are some usual needs that the at-risk or disabled child shares with all children, as well as needs related to the child's special status. An IFSP for any child should consider the relative balance of usual and special needs in assessing what should be offered, as well as how, where, and when the services should be delivered.

*Health care needs* in the at-risk and disabled child encompass ordinary needs such as vaccinations, well-child checkups, and care for acute illnesses. Also included is care related to disabling conditions, such as in the monitoring of kidney and bladder function in a child with spina bifida, or extraordinary long-term medical care related to the child's special status. One example of this would be hospitalization and follow-up of a very premature infant. While it is still common for people to associate disability with illness, statistics show that it is a rather small number of people with disabilities who have extraordinary health care needs. The need for disability-related health care services is by no means universal among the population of at-risk and disabled children.

Four major areas of *developmental need* that are of concern include socioemotional, cognitive, communication, and sensorimotor development. All children need support, either through formal education or natural experience and contacts, for development in these areas. This support may be available to the at-risk and disabled child in ordinary ways, through family interactions and community experiences such as day care or preschool. In some cases, the child's status may call for modest professional effort, such as offering parents guidance in handling and carrying a child. For the child with severe or multiple disabilities, developmental needs may be such that many special efforts must be made, for example, home visits by therapists, frequent center-based contacts, and extensive parent participation in therapy.

Subsumed under the label *family needs* are those broad-based needs that pertain to the child's family environment, such as food, shelter, and employment, rather than to the child's particular needs. All families, for example, need social support. Normally, this need is met within the context of community and family associations. For the family with an at-risk or disabled child, this kind of usual support may not be enough; parents may need access to other parents of children with disabilities or to special counseling, for example. Also included here are such special family needs as money to buy equipment for a child with a disability, special day care for a child with working parents, or information about Medicaid for the family overwhelmed by hospital expenses.

The section of the IFSP that deals with the assessment of family strengths and needs and with goal setting for families represents a critical new element, even for those states that have previously developed IEPs for children from birth. The law calls for a "statement of family strengths and needs relating to enhancing the development of the family's handicapped infant or toddler."

The IFSP is a concrete reflection of our understanding of the key influence of the family on the child, but it also raises major concerns as details are explored. One relates to the ethics of "assessing" families. What will this mean? Will questions be asked about use of alcohol? Who sleeps in what beds? Will families feel they have to reveal intimate details in order for a child to receive services? As one home visit professional states: "If I have to assess families like I assess children, I will quit my job."

The other major issue concerns the scope of the law. We know, for example, that alcoholism in a parent can have an important effect on a child's development. But even if a parent is interested, will alcohol treatment be part of the IFSP? And if it is, who is mandated to find and pay for these services? The meaning of the *family needs* component of the IFSP will be an important focus as details of implementation evolve. "I feel the family component is very worthy" says one parent. "But I have concerns that it appears to promise too much. These things that families need are often not available and this legislation can't provide all that is missing."

Every family with an at-risk or disabled child will have a different profile of strengths and needs. But directing services toward a family simply because a child has a labeled disability is not only a misuse of scarce resources, but runs counter to the goal of maximizing the independence of both families and children. In looking at family profiles, the principles of normalization should apply. A need, even a special need, does not necessarily have to be met by special services. A family may have a need for extra support because of the status of a child, but they may get that special support as a matter of course and choice from the community, for example, through church affiliation.

## HOW PROGRAMS CAN INFLUENCE DEVELOPMENT

Early intervention goals can range from efforts that are actually intended to correct something that *is* wrong to efforts that are meant to protect and encourage good things that are already happening. *Intervention* becomes *interference* when it hinders parents from developing confidence, or when it needlessly limits a parent's intuitive interactions with a child. Goals can be grouped roughly as follows: 1) monitoring progress, 2) prevention and assurance efforts, 3) therapeutic efforts, 4) compensatory efforts, 5) supplementary efforts, and 6) maintenance efforts.

*Monitoring progress* of the at-risk child and his or her family can serve to reassure parents and other family members that the child is doing well and does not need to be involved in a special developmental program. Family intuitions about a child's need for social and educational experiences beyond the family setting (e.g., day care, nursery-preschool, church programs, public and private social agency activities) can be supported, and health, developmental, and social screening information can be collected at periodic intervals for use by both parents and professionals.

*Prevention and assurance efforts* can encourage and support parents when the child is doing well in spite of some discernible disability. A child with cerebral palsy may have motor delays but may be functioning normally in other developmental areas. The parents, however, may see the child's development in a more negative light than is warranted. Goals may relate to involving parents more with the child's positive capacities, or encouraging parents to become involved with a parent group.

*Therapeutic efforts* are designed to eliminate or reduce a deficit. A child who has spasticity may sit with abnormal posture. Direct therapy designed to inhibit abnormal muscle tone and promote more normalized balance, movement, and body alignment is an example of a therapeutic effort. The home use of supplemental oxygen for a premature baby with continuing lung problems is also an example of therapeutic intervention.

*Compensatory efforts* attempt to build an alternative to a deficit that probably can't be corrected. Teaching sign language to a child whose oral language is not functional would be an example of a compensatory effort.

*Supplementary efforts* are meant to add normal kinds of experiences in an environment that is suboptimal or abnormal. These efforts apply, for example, to the infant in intensive care for whom special efforts must be made for parents to do usual things, such as touch and talk to their child.

*Maintenance efforts* are aimed at keeping a child's status from regressing. For a child with language delay who also has serious cognitive and motor delay, the goal of intervention may be to help the child maintain social interactions. For a very young child who is achieving some independence in self-feeding and exploratory play who must undergo orthopedic surgery, a maintenance goal may be to encourage the child's ongoing abilities as much as possible while health concerns are being resolved.

Although at-risk and disabled children have special needs, they also have needs common to all children. These common needs may be intensified because of vulnerabilities. All infants, for example, need opportunities for interaction with caregivers. The at-risk or disabled child may be especially vulnerable to failure in these transactions because that child may not have typical infant behaviors that engage caregivers, and because caregivers may find some of the child's behaviors difficult to interpret.

Program goals and activities for a particular child should be based on a careful evaluation of needs, not just the needs of the child but of the family as a whole. It is a common criticism of efficacy studies that they are still measuring outcomes related primarily to the development of the child. The most commonly measured outcome is cognitive development. There are strong feelings that efficacy measures should rest not just on change in the development of the child, but on the balance of change and adjustment in both the child and family. Not only do we need to improve socioemotional, cognitive, communication, and sensorimotor development in at-risk and disabled children, we also need to better understand and be able to assess the more difficult to measure outcomes related to family adjustment and coping abilities. (See bibliographies, category F, for related references.)

The IFSP is an obvious first step. It is, however, a delicate and difficult task to achieve, especially given the caseloads of some professionals. An accurate assessment of strengths and needs may require an inconvenient investment of time in observing, or getting to know, the family and child. Categorical plans are more convenient but less individualized. A child with moderate physical disability from a low income family gets Plan A, the child with mental retardation and medical complications gets Plan B. It is more difficult to create an individualized plan that considers not only what the child needs, but also what the family's strengths and vulnerabilities are, and that takes into consideration the effects of bringing an outsider into the situation. All at-risk and disabled children may not need direct developmental programming, but it takes the same process of observation to find that a child and family don't need services as it does to find out what services they do need.

## Parent Participation

The value of parent participation in efforts to influence a child's development has been well established through PL 99-457. The goals of parent participation cover many areas, and include:

Meeting the legal rights of the parent to be informed and to make decisions
Using parent input to help establish functional goals for the child
Having parents share "home-based" information about the child
Enlisting the parents' aid in programs to be carried out in the home
Improving the parental sense of competence and the quality of parent-child interactions

While the goals are all sound, their achievement in birth to three practices has been uneven. In states that have used IEP meetings in the past with children from birth, parent participation has not been optimal. Many parents report that going to such meetings is an unpleasant chore. Despite goals to the contrary, the format of the meetings is often one wherein parents are told by professionals what is being done for the child and what the parental role should be. The extent of parent activity in many cases may be only to sign forms. It is often the case that parents will come to the first one or two meetings and then stop coming. Often, these meetings are not favorite experiences for professionals either. They may find it difficult to encourage parents to talk, or may find that those who do talk seem belligerent and demanding. PL 94-142 has given us ample experience with these problems and the new law offers opportunities for change.

The structure for parent participation in early intervention programs may vary. When direct therapeutic efforts are involved, it may be the professional who acts, while the parent either watches or goes off to do something else. Parent involvement in the assessment and intervention processes should be provided for and supported administratively, not trusted to chance. "Administratively" cannot mean simply "written down." The concept must also be supported and demonstrated in preservice training programs; beyond the training level, there must be a vehicle for ensuring that the principles learned are put into practice. This is, at times, a delicate task. Inservice training should involve parents as well as professionals. Professionals need guidance, but parents also need to learn how to break their roles as recipients and to collaborate with professionals.

## SUMMARY

In this chapter, we have explored some fundamental ideas that should be considered in sound developmental programs for at-risk and disabled children. Without getting into specifics of techniques or lesson plans, we outline ideas that offer guidance in establishing programs that are both consistent with what is known about child development processes and about the importance of the family environment. These ideas include the following:

1. While distinctions between socioemotional, cognitive, communication, and sensorimotor development, or between developmental, health, and family needs may always be somewhat artificial, they are especially difficult to consider separately in the very young child.
2. In each of the three main areas of needs, health, development, and family, there are some needs that the at-risk or disabled child shares with all children, as well as needs related to the child's special status. An IFSP should consider the relative balance of usual and special needs in assessing

what services are needed, as well as how, where, and when they should be delivered.

3. A primary aspect of development programs is a process of careful observation that allows for continual assessment of changing needs and creative ways to meet them. Things such as curriculum guides, developmental checklists, and materials, must *serve* this process, not determine what it is.

4. Intervention goals and activities for a particular child should be based on a careful evaluation of strengths and needs, not just those of the child, but of the family as a whole.

5. The needs of any particular child or family will often fall under the category of "vulnerability" rather than outright "disability"; associated program goals may not be to directly influence child change, but to support and encourage the natural strengths of the family.

6. The separation of assessment and intervention activities, whether administratively or methodologically, is artificial and often counterproductive.

7. Ways to effectively assess adaptive development of children who are at-risk or disabled are not yet well established. Careful observation and creativity on the part of parents and professionals will be needed to define such assessment procedures.

8. Assessment and intervention processes should involve concern for the quality of behaviors, not just their presence or absence. The circumstances under which a desired behavior occurs, for example, how, when, and in what manner, should direct future programming.

9. Parent collaboration in assessment and intervention processes should be provided for and supported administratively, not trusted to chance.

10. Development programs may involve dealing directly with parents to support parent-child interactions along with, or instead of, direct involvement with the child.

11. The efficacy of development programs should not be judged by change in the development of the child alone, but also by the success of the support offered for the family's adaptation to life with a child with special needs.

We have discussed briefly some of the issues that should be considered in evaluating the effectiveness of early intervention programs. While goals related to family support now more frequently complement the original child-centered goals of early intervention, progress toward any program goal will not be determined alone by how well early intervention professionals do their work. The next chapter will focus on social attitudes and policy as they relate to the family, and specifically to the care of at-risk and disabled children. Several of the elements of the broad social environment in which early intervention programs must function and gather support are outlined.

# Chapter 5

# Social Attitudes/
# Social Policy

This chapter discusses issues of social attitudes and social policy that have particular relevance for early intervention services, including:

- **the relationship between research and policy formation**
- **signs of progress in services for people with disabilities**
- **national views on social programs**
- **socioeconomic risk**
- **family support**
- **the attraction of high technology approaches to service**
- **policies toward care for children**
- **barriers to interdisciplinary functioning**
- **the need for advocacy efforts**

*A* pediatrician is processing insurance papers for a family with a disabled child. The child needs a wheelchair, and the physician prescribes a lightweight and relatively expensive chair because the child is cared for primarily by a somewhat frail grandmother. The insurance com-

*pany will only pay for the heavy, less expensive chair because it meets the child's needs adequately.*

*A young couple has an infant with severe disabilities, among them chronic and complex medical problems. They move from a small town to a city where the child can receive medical services. The father loses his insurance benefits in changing jobs. The mother cannot go to work because it would keep the family from qualifying for Medicaid. They qualify for food stamps, but the mother will not use them because she finds the stares of other shoppers humiliating.*

*A charitable group in a small city meets to decide on an appropriate community service project to fund. A recommendation comes from a county social worker that funding should go to a respite care program for the parents of children with disabilities, which would offer regular relief from caregiving activities. The group chooses instead to contribute to a fund for a computerized axial tomography (CAT) scanner for the local hospital.*

So far in this book, we have emphasized the complex needs of the very young, at-risk or disabled child, and the intimate and interpersonal nature of the professionals' involvement with such children and with their families. This highly individualized approach to early intervention must, however, be set in the context of social policy and social attitudes. For even the most energetic and committed parents and professionals, transactions with the broader workings of society can be difficult and frustrating.

The study of policy formation is an emerging discipline that offers ways to understand and possibly influence the use of public resources. It is also an area of study that lends itself to biased interpretation by political causes and special interest groups. Views about the nature of social policy concerning services for at-risk and disabled children range from the definitive belief that we are struggling in a worthy but doomed effort, to the belief that policy is clearly moving toward the support of improved services. The passage of PL 99-457 supports the latter view. This law is a major statement that it is in our national interest to nourish the potential in young children with disabilities through early services. The new law is, however, only one piece of our policy puzzle.

We will, for the most part, refer to *social* policy rather than *public* policy, as the latter seems more directly tied to government policies. What will be reflected here are themes that are not tied to government actions alone, but to broader social issues and attitudes that influence the service environment. These themes reflect present barriers and support for the mission of PL 99-457.

Indices of social policy are varied. Social policy is seen as directing priorities and activities in human services programs, either at the national, state, or local level. Policy is reflected strongly in legislative actions, as well as in the judicial system, which interprets and enforces legislation. Social policy is a reflection of the current values of our culture. Election results and public opinion polls provide indicators of social policy. But, although some resist its simplicity, the most concrete measure of policy is financial. For many, the best index of social policy is "who gets money for what." Themes explored in this chapter however, will not only be those related to funding for early intervention programs, but also those related to other influential areas, such as attitudes toward the disabled, toward the family, toward children, and toward health, education, and social services.

## RESEARCH AND POLICY

To what extent do the results of research affect legislators and other key personnel involved with laws and funding? Despite the reverence for data in this country, the connection between scientific research and policy formation is not clear. It is evident, however, that the relationship is not a direct one. Even among professionals involved in early intervention, opinions range from a firm belief in the influence of good and timely data, to a cynical belief that it is not facts that run the show at all.

It is largely in the area of preventive efforts and primary care programs that people seem the most discouraged about the relationship between data and policy. Broadly available prenatal and perinatal care programs have been shown to have important effects in reducing premature births, the number of low birth weight infants, and a number of other risk factors. Yet it is generally these broad-based "noncrisis" programs that are cut first when budgets are tight. In a similar light, programs that make health care available to families, particularly low income families, have been shown to be cost-effective in terms of appropriate use of health care. But these programs are also vulnerable, and tend to come and go with changes in the economic and philosophical climate.

On the positive side, both the evidence drawn from research findings and an improved level of public awareness have contributed to some growth in policy commitments for early intervention services, including the passage of PL 99-457. If it is to effectively influence policy, research must be used to answer appropriate questions. Research cannot resolve the issue of whether or not a society should provide special help to at-risk or disabled children and their families, but it can answer questions about how such a commitment, once made, is best accomplished, and at what cost.

## HISTORICAL PROGRESS

The social climate that currently surrounds early intervention services, while not ideal, is dramatically improved from past years. Although the connection between policy and research is an uncertain one, the revolution in services for persons with disabilities provides an arena in which science and public attitudes are related in hopeful ways. There is considerable optimism, most strongly among professionals and parents, about what can be done for at-risk and disabled children.

Only a few years ago, routine institutionalization was the acceptable public method of service provision for children who had obvious disabilities at birth or as young children. Similarly, it has only been a few years since education for children with disabilities, if available at all, was provided in segregated facilities. Residential facilities, whether overcrowded and underfunded public ones, or more comfortable private ones, were isolated from the community.

Today, the routine institutionalization of children with disabilities would shock us. It has been found that, for the most part, children do better in the home environment. With support, it is also possible for families to adjust and even thrive with their children at home. However, some families will need alternatives to caring for their child at home, either because of the child's status or because of the particular family ecology. For these families, the alternative to keeping the child at home can involve various placement options in which the child can be well nurtured. Increasingly, these are located in community settings where family involvement does not have to be totally cut off. There is support for this move because of the outcomes for the children, but there is also a sense that this is a better way for us all to live, and that this is more the kind of society we were meant to be.

"I feel," offers the father of a severely disabled child, "that society, at least the people I know, is becoming very accepting of children who have special problems. When I was a child there were no handicapped children in my school, and yet I know there must have been some in town. They must have been sent away because I never saw one. My son goes to a regular elementary school. There are special classes for him, but also activities where all the kids do things together. I think people are changing."

Progress in service provision for the child who is labeled biologically "at risk," as opposed to being discernibly disabled, has been of a somewhat different nature, as the survival rate for these children has changed dramatically, and continues to change. The optimism surrounding these children comes from technology that has made it possible for them to live, as well as from increasing evidence suggesting that with supportive family and services, the vast majority of such children can develop normally.

Progress concerning policies toward children at environmental and/or socioeconomic risk is still a gray area. While it has been shown that early intervention can have a positive impact on the detrimental effects of poverty, policy-wise we are still involved in a national argument over how poverty should be "treated." Children are the innocent victims of the argument, whether or not they are also biologically at risk or discernibly handicapped.

## NATIONAL VIEWS ON SOCIAL PROGRAMS

Attitudes that influence the way early intervention services are made available are strongly tied to national views about social programs in general. Two influential themes on social programs are in an uneasy and variable state of coexistence. These themes have direct bearing on policy toward services for at-risk and disabled children, and on policy related to family support efforts. One theme pictures social programs as a proper expression of "being our brother's keeper"; the other theme pictures social programs as eroding the child's potential for self-sufficiency, for self-regulation, and for individual triumph over adversity. Each view has deep roots in the history of our culture; combined, they represent a debate over the cause and effect relationship between an individual's actions and the need to turn to public programs for help. Will social programs tend to strengthen people and make them more productive citizens, or will social programs contribute to a cycle of dependence?

The tug and pull of these views has a number of important direct effects on families with an at-risk or disabled child. While few would directly suggest today that the presence of disability is a sign of some character weakness in the parents or in the child, traces of this belief are still influential. Parents commonly react to the arrival of an at-risk and disabled child with guilt, and a powerful sense of having done something wrong despite all objective facts to the contrary. This guilt is compounded when parents must ask for help. It is compounded even further when asking is not enough, and a full-blown crisis is required to gain access to needed services.

Another effect of the tug and pull of philosophies is that there is not a great deal of stability to the direction of social programs. When the "brother's keeper" philosophy is ascendant, programs are more abundant, and less difficult to qualify for, and the social stigma attached to participating is less. When "self-sufficiency" reigns, programs are lost or cut back, and criteria for participation are made more stringent. "We live with an axe over us," says one administrator. "Instead of accepting the premise of our program and helping us improve, it seems people are looking for excuses to pull back. Almost yearly we have to develop a caucus of physicians and other people with political contacts to say: 'Yes, they are doing a good job; yes, prevention is something important.' "

## FAMILY SUPPORT

The strong and broad family support element in PL 99-457 is a bold statement in a weak area of American public policy. There is still a common belief that public programs are for families that have failed. Parents who are already, in many cases, questioning their worth for having a disabled child at all, must in addition cope with the sometimes not-so-hidden condemnation implied in asking for services. One woman from an upper-middle-class family was caught between insurance policies when her daughter was born 3 months early. Massive medical bills forced the family to apply for Medicaid. When the social worker arrived at her home in a van marked "Department of Social Services," the mother was overwhelmed and surprised by her own feelings of shame. Another mother of a severely disabled child in elementary school was confronted by an annoyed neighbor. "Our kids are going without new football uniforms and your kid is getting everything," she was told.

Certain policies affecting access to programs may actually promote failures. Some families must adjust their personal and financial aspirations downward in order to maintain their qualifications for services. Competitive access to early intervention programs can force families to convince authorities that they can't cope. Progress, either in the family's finances or in the child's status, may be penalized with the loss of access to particular programs.

Our tendency is to sacrifice preventive, maintenance, and

support care for more dramatic technological interventions. Cost-effective preventive and supportive care available routinely in some other countries, such as in Scandinavia, is discretionary in this country. Discretionary standards are usually based on income criteria. In hard economic times, eligibility becomes more restricted, with the result that even persons with lower incomes may lose services. This leaves families with an at-risk or disabled child coping not only with crises related to the child's condition, but often with chronic crises related to how services can be obtained.

In addition to the pressures involved in asking for financial assistance, many parents feel under special scrutiny because of the expectations of "sainthood" that still exist. Some find it is still taboo to complain or joke about the trials of raising a special child, even though such complaints would be acceptable if the child were normal. A decision to use respite care, or to choose residential placement for a child, can be made even more difficult with the added pain of outside criticism.

Resistance to family support is sometimes dramatically costly to society. A mother who was the sole support of her daughter reported her experience in asking for $200 a month in assistance from social services so she could move from a third floor to a ground floor apartment when her daughter started using a wheelchair. The denial of her request forced the mother to send the child to a state supported residential facility at great state expense and emotional cost to the mother and daughter. Cases of insurance companies refusing to pay for home care of chronically ill children are not uncommon and offer a further example of this kind of resistance.

The stigma of asking for help is changing slowly in some areas. Programs that serve some of the functions of social support for parents of at-risk and disabled children are gradually gaining acceptability and permanence. During the seventies, support groups became solid middle-class institutions, and included consciousness-raising groups for men and women, weight loss groups, quit-smoking groups, and coping-with-disease groups. Some high schools now have special programs that are designed to encourage teenage mothers to come back to school, and to provide support for them as parents. Support groups for single parents are a relatively familiar community service, as are crisis lines, programs for latchkey children, and in some communities, a growing public and private commitment to provision of day care.

Needs for early intervention and family social support services do not carry the ominous stigma of "breakdown" they may once have. But family support and improved family functioning may not yet carry a great deal of weight as a rationale for early intervention, despite the commitment of PL 99-457. "I think still the major interest in these programs, as a whole, is in improving the intellectual functioning of the child," offers a pediatrician. "If we say the payoff is going to be in improved social functioning of families, even if there are financial benefits to society for that, I just don't know if it would sell."

## THE APPEAL OF HIGH TECHNOLOGY

While there is a growing response to children with special needs, the funding is not consistently available for those services felt to be the most effective in promoting optimal outcomes. Public interest and support for services for at-risk and disabled children centers on crisis-oriented, high tech care and solutions. Working with families to solve chronic problems, although necessary to improve long-term outcomes, does not excite great interest as a policy issue. Our national love of technology has many facets. One of them is monetary. High tech efforts are financially rewarding for some practitioners, facilities, and manufacturers. Society as a whole, even when paying the price for this orientation, likes high tech solutions and believes in them. As one clinician commented: "Television would cover a dramatic heart surgery for a premature baby. They wouldn't do a feature on the weeks of work with parents, child, and therapist to get a child to use a cup, or to teach feeding techniques so a child won't gag." Relatively recent polls have shown that, despite skyrocketing health costs, the areas that the public would cut first are preventive and maintenance care, as well as health programs that reach the poor.

While the love of technology is most visible in the health care setting, it has strong components in the area of developmental programming as well. Technological advances designed to improve the lives of people with disabilities are important. Mobility devices, communication devices, and computers can all contribute to independence and improved quality of life for persons with disabilities. But technology clearly needs to be sensibly and sensitively used, in combination with other kinds of efforts. The fast-paced drama of technological effort must be synchronized with the slow-paced and arduous progress that is the hallmark of work with special needs children. And developmental progress is only part of the picture. Persons with disabilities and their families have reported over and over that it is loneliness and social isolation that is their most overwhelming handicapping condition. These needs must be addressed by social policy along with the practical needs associated with physical care of the child.

## POLICIES FOR CHILDREN AND FAMILIES

"In terms of services," says a program administrator, "it is clear that if you want to serve certain people with disabilities, it's possible because people can *see* the need; they know we must serve our disabled and our elderly. But if you want to do any kind of prevention or identification or support, that becomes less tangible. What it gets down to is that the United States does not have a policy for children the way, say, a country like Japan does, or France, or Israel. When you talk to people in these countries, they cannot believe we do not have a policy for children, for every child, because children to them are a good investment. If you offer early intervention to a child, or if you offer all women prenatal care without reference to financial status, this is seen as an excellent means of ensuring that the future generation will be a good one."

The status of child care services in the United States illustrates the absence of a national policy for children. Despite the increasing numbers of preschool-age children who must be in day care because of working parents, progress in child care has been notably slow. One reason is that we are still reluctant to tamper with the image of the American family that assumes a mother stays home to care for her children.

If quality day care is difficult to find for normal children, it is close to impossible to find for children with special needs. The parent who wants or needs to go to work is in a difficult position. "I'm on the board of directors of a center that has just been funded to provide day care for medically fragile infants," says an NICU nurse. "I mean, it gradually dawned on us that we were sending these babies home from the neonatal unit with mothers who *had* to work. We are often talking about desperate situations: families swamped by bills who may lose their homes without the mother working. And who will take a sick baby all hung with tubes"? While many modern stresses, including psychological, financial, and marital stresses, are more pronounced in the family with special needs, the mother is largely denied the opportunity to find financial or psychological relief through work. Relief for parents, either in the form of respite care, or in the form of more day care for children with special needs, should be part of improving the home environment for the at-risk or disabled child.

For the parent (usually the mother) who does stay home with the child with a disability, strenuous routines, such as medical visits, special feedings, and therapies, may fill the days with obligations but may not provide the traditional rewards inherent in caring for a normal child. This puts enormous pressure on mothers who cannot live up to the unrealistic societal expectation that they will have endless patience; for these mothers, asking for help is seen as a sign of failure. For the most part, families who raised their disabled child in uncomplaining isolation in the past did not do so because they were extraordinary people, or because they didn't feel they needed help. These families were silent because, even when help was available, the price of asking for it was too great. This is still true for many families.

An additional problem concerns child care staff. Despite what we have learned about the complex development of the young child, there is still a belief that child care is something that takes little skill. This means that child care workers are notoriously underpaid, even in settings where staff have degrees in early childhood education.

Although much is asked of them in terms of their own investment in training, skilled professionals in early intervention are modestly paid. "I get discouraged when I hear how social services don't pay anything," says one therapist. "I have a friend who supplies coffee for television studios, and he made $60,000 last year. I can't help feeling that's not fair. But it's just the way money produces certain incomes and this is not seen as a money producing business. We know we are saving money, but we're not reimbursed." As state legislatures look seriously at standards for early intervention personnel and at the plan for personnel development called for in PL 99-457, the gap between what personnel are expected to know and do, and what they are paid, must be addressed.

## INTERDISCIPLINARY ENVIRONMENT

Our individualistic and competitive society, when transposed into individualistic and competitive professional groups, creates a difficult environment for the development of the interdisciplinary process. While many service providers use "teamwork" in their goals, real egalitarian teamwork is likely to be the occasional product of particular personal combinations rather than something that is consistently achieved by design.

These individualistic and competitive qualities translate into policies and attitudes that affect services for at-risk and disabled children in several ways. As society is inclined to direct funding toward dramatic high tech efforts, so it is also inclined to reward professionals for individual efforts that are highly visible. The occupational therapist who consistently spends extra time talking to families may not be doing other, more visible, tasks. For example, the therapist may not be completing paperwork, or may not be publishing journal articles, or may not be developing new devices for improving daily care routines. The special, less visible or dramatic interpersonal rewards that come from such an investment of time are enough for some, but they may cause other professionals to experience burnout.

Despite the need for an interdisciplinary approach to resolving the problems of the at-risk or disabled child, and his or her family, legislative funding policies generally have not accommodated this need. Thus, the education agency looking after the developmental needs of a disabled child may have no administrative structure or motivation for getting involved with the pediatrician or with the social service agency that is involved with the family. There is a tendency to be possessive about cases, even though work loads may be heavy, since financial reward and a sense of professional competence go to the person or agency to whom the child "belongs." Efforts to combat this separatism are sometimes blocked administratively. For example, one state professional board may not allow continuing education credit for a speech-language pathologist to attend a nursing conference regarding early health concerns that affect the behavior of premature infants. Similarly, a nursing board may not award such credit to a nurse attending a speech pathology–sponsored conference regarding early communication between infants and their parents.

PL 99-457 mandates the inclusion of parents and the incorporation of multiple disciplines in developing the IFSP, and interagency collaboration in providing and paying for services. These mandates should have a significant impact on the interdisciplinary environment.

## NEED FOR ADVOCACY

While social policy and social attitudes present problems for early intervention services, we have begun to understand how effective services can be put together. As with many social programs, however, early intervention will sail into the foreseeable future on various economic and social tides. It is clear, for example, that changes in the political and economic climate can result in reversals of positive changes in care and attitudes. The advocacy alliance of professionals and parents that resulted in the passage of PL 99-457 must be maintained to avoid such a reversal. "I think one real important point that's sort of emerging is that when programs for disabled children are created, it's because parents demand them," says one practitioner. "It's not a group of administrators sitting around saying: 'Oh, we need this.' Change comes when the people that need the services finally say: 'We want this. We're part of the community. We're taxpayers.' That's how we're going to get through to the decision makers."

---

**A social worker says: "I had some experience with one national parent group, and they had worked for years trying to change things for kids as a strictly parent group. Then they moved into a new phase where they would invite professionals to join their group, and they have found that they have been able to effect more change with this team approach, parents and professionals together."**

---

As professionals and parents join forces as advocates, the selling points of early intervention will need to be strengthened. This will require support for research and documentation of the effectiveness of services. Also, it will require vivid individual success stories that will speak to humanitarian interests.

As some advocates have learned, it is effective and appropriate to remind people that anyone can be touched by the need for early intervention. "I speak to service clubs," reports one administrator. "I mean, I don't do a big suction for dollars, but I try to share information, answer questions like: 'Well, what *do* you teach a baby?' I had a fellow come up to me recently after one of these talks and he said: 'You spoke to this group last year, but I never dreamed I would need your services.' He and his wife had just had a child with Cornelia de Lange syndrome. So, you see, we are really all at risk."

It might seem impossible now that our society could revert to less enlightened views of the importance of supporting development in the very young child. A movement backward may not seem likely. There are committed professionals who have had years to witness the importance of early intervention efforts. There are parents who have had children enrolled in programs since birth who do not know about life before Public Law 94-142 and the commitments involved in making it come to pass. There is a surge of interest around PL 99-457, but many warn that without the vigilance of concerned individuals, important gains may be lost. Among other things, the history of social policy shows that this vigilance does make a difference. (See bibliographies, category H, for related references.)

## SUMMARY

In this chapter, we have discussed the major themes of social attitudes and policy concerning services for at-risk and disabled children. These themes include the following:

1.  Two coexisting national views of social programs affect policy toward early intervention for at-risk and disabled children and policy related to family support efforts. One view sees social programs as society's proper expression of the philosophy of "being our brother's keeper"; the other view sees social programs as eroding the child's potential for self-sufficiency, self-regulation, and individual triumph over adversity.

2.  In the current balance of these views, there is still an important underlying public belief that government only steps in when families fail. However, programs that serve some of the functions of social support are gradually gaining acceptability and permanence.

3.  Despite the reverence for data in our society, it is not clear what role scientific research plays in influencing policy, although it is evident that, overall, this relationship is not a direct one. It is also apparent, however, that more efforts to collect relevant data concerning early intervention are needed.

4.  Although the connection between policy and research is gen-

erally an uncertain one, the change in attitudes toward and services for persons with disabilities provides an arena in which science and public attitudes are related in promising ways. As a result, there is considerable optimism about what can be done for at-risk children and children with disabilities.

5. Public interest and support for services for at-risk and disabled children often center on crisis-oriented, high tech care and solutions. Working with families on chronic problems does not excite great interest as a policy issue.

6. Certain kinds of preventive and maintenance care that are available routinely in most other industrialized countries are discretionary in this country. This means that families with an at-risk or disabled child must sometimes struggle to prove they are "disadvantaged enough" to receive services.

7. The commonly held attitude that child care is unskilled labor does not provide a favorable atmosphere in which to develop programs that offer support and training for the complex task of caring for an at-risk or disabled child.

8. Our individualistic and competitive society is a difficult environment for the development of the interdisciplinary process.

9. It is clearly possible that changes in the political and economic climate can result in reversals of recent progress in attitudes about service provision. The advocacy alliance of professionals and parents must be maintained if such a loss is to be avoided.

These themes illustrate some potential barriers to the individualized, family-oriented and transactional approach to early intervention services that has been described so far. What organizational considerations are needed to integrate the intimate quality of early intervention into a method of service delivery? Among professionals and agencies with a strong sense of turf, what service delivery factors promote the kind of coordination that is essential to effective and efficient early intervention? What factors can promote the flexibility needed to support families with a special needs child? In the next chapter, we outline some major organizational considerations in service delivery.

## Chapter 6

# Service Delivery and Organizational Considerations

This chapter describes the elements of service delivery and organizational factors that must be considered in creating an effective service system, including:

- **the services needed**
- **the influence of attitudes and social policy**
- **preservice and inservice training**
- **the research-practice exchange**
- **service coordination**
- **case management**
- **national and state mandates**
- **decision-making processes**
- **the individual's role in change**

hile recent years have brought great improvements in services for all persons with disabilities, access to *quality interdisciplinary* services is still uneven. Exemplary programs may be available in one state, but only in a particular urban area, leaving residents of rural areas scrambling to find services that are barely adequate. Similarly, innovative and successful programs may be available in special education but not in vocational training, or in residential programs for mentally retarded persons but not for physically disabled individuals. Program admission criteria may discriminate on grounds of severity of disability, diagnostic categories, potential for rehabilitation, or economic status of the family.

## SERVICE DELIVERY FOR AT-RISK AND DISABLED CHILDREN

Because programs for very young at-risk and disabled children are relatively new, this uneven availability is especially acute in these services. Before the passage of PL 99-457, some states had mandated early intervention services at birth, other states had some services, still others had nothing. It is painful for parents to know that good things are happening in the next town or county or state, but not for their child. Awareness of how important the early years are to optimal development creates an added sorrow for those who must do without services.

PL 99-457 defines early intervention as including:

Family training, counseling, and home visits
Special instruction
Speech-language pathology and audiology
Occupational therapy
Physical therapy
Psychological services
Case management services
Medical services for diagnostic or evaluation purposes
Early identification, screening, and assessment services
Health services necessary to enable the infant and toddler to benefit from other intervention services

How will the system as a whole function? How does the child move from being unidentified to receiving appropriate services? How do we keep services appropriate as child and family needs change? How do we stay in touch with children who are at risk but who are not currently in need of services? In this chapter, we present an outline of the functions that need to be in place. Organizational elements that influence these functions are also considered.

This document has emphasized personal interaction as a critical element in making things work. We have stressed that services need to be individualized, based on careful scientific observation of the strengths and needs of the child and family, and that the child's family environment must be seen as a major component in programming efforts. The ability to carry out this individualized and interpersonal approach depends on numerous factors. One is the degree to which a child's therapeutic and developmental needs are compounded by other needs of the family, including socioeconomic needs. Another factor is the degree of support, both financial and administrative, available for the practitioner involved in these interpersonal, family-centered efforts. The practitioner cannot act alone: effective interventions for families with complex problems can only be approached by coordinated interagency efforts.

## The Coordination of Interagency Efforts

Just as the services themselves are of an interpersonal nature, the building of a system in which they can function should also be an individualized effort. It should be based on the difficult forging of inter- and intraprofessional relationships as well as interagency contacts. Services need to be interdisciplinary not just in the sense of the various disciplines involved in a single program, but also interdisciplinary in terms of the communication between agencies and organizations concerned with the child and family.

The new legislation has sketched a service organization by identifying a lead agency in each state, and an interagency coordinating council with representatives from those elements who will need to collaborate. State legislatures have been given ample room to build organizations to fit their individual strengths and needs.

Prevention, identification, referral, confirmation/diagnosis, assessment, planning delivery, transition, evaluation, tracking, and exiting are some of the functions that the early intervention system may need to have in place. As a community or state service system is assessed for strengths and weaknesses, the status of these elements may point out where new energy must be focused to strengthen or create new programs.

*Prevention*    Efforts to prevent disabilities can be classified into three areas. *Primary prevention* focuses on efforts to actually prevent high-risk conditions or disabilities. *Secondary prevention* includes efforts to identify problems early, so that an existing condition can be corrected or its effects minimized. *Tertiary prevention* focuses on efforts to provide health care and rehabilitative services so that an established disability does not become more severe or bring on the burden of other disabilities.

Family planning is seen by many as a first priority in prevention efforts, and as a way to ensure that all children are wanted. Prepregnancy counseling and genetic counseling are a growing part of prevention efforts. More and more, we see the emotional state of the parents, especially the mother, as having an important effect on the unborn child. Prenatal care, and the nutrition counseling and parenting education that go with it, are also critical elements in primary prevention. A primary early intervention effort would be to ensure that those parents whose children are most at risk, for example, teenage mothers and parents in low socioeconomic circumstances, have access to such services.

Also of concern are efforts aimed at preventing failures in social development for children already born with vulnerabilities or existing limitations. Most children born with biological risk factors do develop normally. However, there is a range of potential developmental outcomes within many diagnostic categories of disability, making the issue of prevention a salient one. Social support for families, especially support for the relationship between children and parents, is felt to be a preventive strategy in risk situations. The hope of early intervention is to limit the effects of risk factors or disabling conditions as much as possible. Prenatal and perinatal care and other efforts designed to prevent the occurrence of at-risk status lead naturally into the kinds of preventive care that should be available to any child born with a problem. Making it possible for parents and newborn infants to be together as much as possible in the hospital, and emphasizing individualized postpartum follow-up for mothers and infants, are important for all families, but such efforts are especially important for families in at-risk situations.

*Identification*   Identification refers to the screening processes that occur in health and developmental areas. A number of questions need to be asked about screening programs to determine how they fit into the service system as a whole. Except for biologically at-risk infants who are identified immediately in hospital settings, most screening will occur out of the hospital; screening can be done through health, social service, or educational agencies, or through private care and service organizations. While PL 99-457 mandates screening, it leaves flexibility in defining developmental delay and in choosing whether to serve children at risk. These state policy decisions will influence the type of screening that is done. The new law also calls for an identification of all these resources for a statewide directory. Are agencies duplicating efforts in reaching the same children, and are some children not being reached by any of the programs?

In most cases, it is the parents who first sense that a child has a problem. Although parents may resist specific diagnostic labels, they often know something is amiss before professionals do, and especially before professionals are willing to share their concern openly. Attentiveness to and respect for parents' observations can be a primary element in alleviating the frustration and prolonged fear that the identification phase of services often imposes on families. Screening information is the cornerstone of this effort. Without acknowledgment that, yes, there may be a problem, or a potential problem, the process cannot continue.

*First Referral*   The first referral is made from screening-identification to a more complete diagnostic evaluation. The timing between the referral and the diagnostic appointment can be important to the child's health and development, as well as to the family's well-being. If months pass between the referral and the evaluation, the family's introduction to the service system may produce anxiety, as the excessive amount of time permits families to nourish their fears.

*Confirmation/Diagnosis* The point at which the diagnosis is made can be the time when families are most vulnerable, and when the interpersonal nature of the process is most critical. Whether there is a concrete diagnosis, such as cerebral palsy, or there is recognition of a "developmental delay," it is a time that parents often recall for the rest of their lives. "Those first 2 weeks were a nightmare for me," says one mother. "The professionals had to be my friends first, not physicians or physical therapists. I needed them. It took me 2 weeks before I could tell my husband, 6 weeks before I told my mother, and to this day I have not used the term cerebral palsy in front of my mother-in-law." Since diagnostic settings are often not community settings, contact between community and secondary or tertiary personnel is especially important during this time.

*Second Referral* The second referral can direct the parent from the confirmation and diagnosis setting to either the program where actual intervention services are provided or to additional assessment settings to indicate what specific programming would be appropriate. These assessment and program services may be handled by one agency, or may involve the actions of several. If the educational agency has provided the diagnostic evaluation, internal referrals may be made to particular programs within that agency. If a tertiary medical setting has been involved with the diagnosis, then there may need to be special efforts to promote interagency communication that will serve the child appropriately.

*Assessment* Unlike diagnosis, the assessment involves the consideration of specific program content and process. This first assessment stage should be part of an ongoing assessment and programming continuum while the child is receiving services (see Chapter 4).

*Planning* Planning deals with interpretation, translation, and application of diagnostic and assessment information. Practical, meaningful support and services for very young children and their families require that the fewest people deliver the most accurate information possible at the time when it is most needed by parents. Professionals need to communicate with each other, and with the parents, to see that services are responsive to needs, flexible, and consistent.

*Delivery* Delivery involves participation by the child and/or family in actual support services. Placement should not be static, but part of an ongoing process of program adjustment. "The parents and I will start off by writing down some goals that seem to fit with assessment results," says one teacher. "After I relate to the child for a couple of weeks in services, we often need to go back and revise the whole thing and begin again with what is really going to meet the needs of this child. It's not a linear process from a single assessment to an appropriate program plan."

*Transition* "Transition" refers not to *one* element of service but to the repeated passage of the child and family from one set of service circumstances to another. Transitions can occur with changes in availability of services or changes in personnel who coordinate or provide services. The need for services may change from, for example, primary health services to developmental services. Developmental change in the child can indicate a change in services is needed. Both eligibility for services and cost of services can lead to transitions as well.

The IFSP calls specifically for a plan to effect the transition of the child between early intervention and preschool services, but transitions in many areas can be difficult for families who have come to rely on certain sets of circumstances for support. Even when the transition is a sign of progress, such as a transition from the NICU to the home, or from direct therapeutic services to supportive efforts, the change can be unsettling. The loss of secure relationships with particular personnel can lead to an emotional crisis for the family.

*Evaluation* Evaluation is the element of service that measures program efficacy, and child and family outcomes. In addition to quantitative data, evaluations should include qualitative information about the nature of change and limitations in children and families. The type of evaluation that is done reflects the degree to which a program or agency focuses on family-centered as well as child-centered outcomes.

*Tracking* Tracking is a way for the early intervention system to monitor the whereabouts and status of children who have been touched by the system, and includes monitoring the service delivery system as a whole. When a child is identified, at age two, in one screening program, is it known whether or not he passed earlier screenings in other programs? Does the system keep tabs on children who shift from having primarily health concerns to developmental concerns? What are the patterns, in the system as a whole, of interagency referral and communication? Are children being lost who are identified early, disappear, and later need services in elementary school?

*Exiting* Exiting is an important and often overlooked element of the service delivery system. There must be a way for a child and family to leave services if questionable conditions or vulnerabilities have been resolved. Keeping children in programs that are no longer appropriate, whether to keep programs filled or as a result of poor monitoring, contradicts the principles of individualized programming and minimal intervention.

These service elements are in place in varying degrees and strengths in different systems. The task at hand is to determine how these elements can be put together effectively. The concepts of transaction and mutual influence provide a useful way to look at the organization of services. Given the elements needed for a continuum of service provision for at-risk and disabled children and their families, what factors determine the quality of the service system as a whole?

## ATTITUDES AND SOCIAL POLICY

Clearly, the personal attitudes of those involved with early intervention have a powerful influence on how services work, regardless of the organizational structures that are in place. The message given to parents and children can be either: "We work with diagnoses," or: "We serve people."

Discussions dealing with social attitudes and policy in Chapter 5 indicate ways that, even with the best individual attitudes among professionals, policies can become barriers to effective service delivery. The national, state, or local priorities that affect the funding of services have a powerful impact not only on the amount that can be spent, but on the sense among professionals and families that there is an ongoing commitment to quality care.

## PRESERVICE TRAINING AND INSERVICE TRAINING

The combination of sensitivity, respect, and expertise called for in early intervention professionals makes the issue of training central to efforts to develop or improve services. The new legislation has appropriately called for the establishment and maintenance of personnel standards and for statewide personnel development plans.

The professional preparation for individualized and family-centered services is of a different kind than that which is aimed solely at disciplinary skill development. We do not know exactly what kind of training will produce the professional needed, but we do know that it will have to involve more exposure to and experience in interdisciplinary efforts, an emphasis on team building and team maintenance skills, a stronger focus on interpersonal and listening skills, and a stronger orientation to observation. There is clearly a limit, however, to the impact of formal training. Many practitioners report that their approaches change dramatically with time and experience. "I think there could be better didactic training," offers one therapist. "But, I don't know how meaningful it is until you work with children and parents. In college, I just don't know if you were thinking about sitting there and having a parent break down in front of you. Maybe there is a way to experience that—I don't know."

Continuing education is especially critical in an area as new and changing as early intervention. Focusing programs on individualized and family-centered support may require the efforts of a professional whose job is essentially continuing education who can act as a facilitator, translator, and prompter for the direct-care providers. While this may seem like a luxury for start-up programs, it can in the long run be an efficient way to bring about needed reorientation and to ensure that practices keep pace with new knowledge.

## RESEARCH-PRACTICE EXCHANGE

The extent to which new information and research reach practicing professionals and to which professionals communicate their concerns to researchers clearly influences the status of services and the effectiveness of both groups. "To really keep up," says one clinician, "you have to read everything: medicine, psychology, genetics, therapies. There's no way. And even when you do read, I find with the professional journals it's awfully difficult to translate into clinical terms. I look at the titles and I think: 'Who cares?' It's not that we're unintelligent or incompetent, but we need some translators between the basic research and the on-line professional."

## COORDINATION

The central directory of available resources and the interagency agreements mandated in PL 99-457 will put weight behind the well-known but vastly underachieved goal of service coordination. When agencies do not work together, fiscal inefficiency, duplication of services, and failure to provide needed services can result. The quality of interagency coordination is affected by the interpersonal relationship between professionals and by administrative structures and regulations. In working toward interagency coordination, it is critical that health care, educational, and social services are all represented. However, the relative commitment of these different service areas may vary, and one service may take a more prominent role than another in putting together programs for the young child.

More than the actual lack of programs, the lack of *awareness* about programs, the lack of a common source of information, and the often conflicting messages from different programs and agencies, are the great service burdens for families. Examples include: the pediatrician who does not know about services provided by a visiting nurse, the visiting nurse who does not know about the support group for parents of premature babies, or the parents' group leader who does not know what Medicaid will and will not cover. "We cared for a child with multiple problems," reports a nurse, "and when the child left the hospital, a number of agencies were involved. We sent reports to the educational unit, to the private agency that was doing physical therapy, and to the medical therapy unit, but I never heard from any of them. I had to get my information from a mother who was illiterate and who never understood what was going on and didn't even know when the child's medical appointments were. It's a frustrating thing. I think there should be a goal somewhere along the line that community agencies who work semi-independently from each have an agreed-upon format for communicating." Overuse, underuse, misuse, and conflict of programs result when concerned parties don't communicate. While funding is always a major issue, service coordination may represent an even more serious barrier to effective delivery of services.

Voluntary community associations such as church, service, and advocacy associations have an important role to play in supportive services, and should be part of service coordination plans. Volunteer associations include service clubs that help to buy equipment for families, church groups providing respite care, and advocacy groups helping to start parent-to-parent support. Some of these groups may offer the best kind of social support, respite care, and other help as part of their social community without having a specific focus on disability service.

## CASE MANAGEMENT ROLES
## AND DETERMINING ACCESS TO PROGRAMS

Who actually coordinates services? Who puts the service plan together and sees that necessary persons are involved and that there is a true understanding of needs and available services? Should parents be service coordinators themselves? Should the case manager be an independent lay ombudsman, or someone such as a social worker who is a member of the agency primarily involved with the child?

The IFSP calls for the case manager to be identified from the profession most immediately relevant to the infant's, toddler's, or family's needs. This person will be responsible for seeing that the IFSP is carried out. Questions are arising about the control that parents will have over this decision, and whether they themselves should serve as case managers.

Access to services is another controversial issue in the service delivery system. Once needs are known, who determines which provider should be used in the system? Who should get what, and where? "It's the eligibility criteria that keep us from developing good individual programs," says one administrator. "You try to send a child to a program with a diagnosis of delay or hypotonia and they laugh in your face. You can't buy anything without a diagnosis of cerebral palsy. But you go to the neurologists and they say: 'Oh no, we won't diagnose cerebral palsy until the child is 3 years old.' So there's all this rigidity and of course it falls on the parents . . . they don't know what to do."

## NATIONAL AND STATE MANDATES

While no one system has emerged, or probably should emerge, to dictate management structures, there is a growing body of experience to be shared about early intervention organizational models. Good interdisciplinary strategies are not abstract ideas, but strategies that have actually worked. Good policy builds from good program history upward. When we know what programs are effective at the community level, it is more feasible to move state policy in that direction. At the same time, the development of uniformly available services cannot occur without supportive state and federal policy mandates.

It is not only inefficient to try to start a whole system from scratch, but in most instances, it does not work. Plans for service delivery need to be built around manageable geographic areas and around service elements that are already in place. If a visiting nurse association is strong and has traditionally been used as liaison between medical and social service personnel, then such a role can be built into newly emerging early intervention programs; if a local physician already has strong ties to the educational system, such a relationship can be included as part of identification efforts. Long-term goals might be to encourage new relationships, but start-up plans should include at least some existing services.

## DECISION MAKING

The ways decisions are made will be a key factor in the quality of early intervention services. A program placement division for a child that does not meaningfully include the parents contains the seeds of failure. The educational system may have excellent ideas for early intervention services in a community. But if a community plan is put in place without the agreement of other parties (e.g., social services, parents, health care personnel), it may never be accepted, no matter how good it is. People who will be needed should be involved from the beginning. They should not be called on to acquiesce to a plan, but to actually shape what that plan will be.

In early intervention, interdisciplinary decision making is the goal. Because of the complex and interrelated needs of at-risk and disabled children, the best decisions about care will be made with the broadest vision. Identifying problems, gathering information, and selecting plans of action are most effective when achieved by consensus, rather than through an authoritarian process. Obtaining a consensus is difficult at best, and programs vary widely in the degree to which they approach the ideal. "From a parent's point of view," says one mother, "you read a lot about interdisciplinary decision-making, but you rarely see it."

In the continuum between authoritarian and consensus forming processes, there are many forces that tend to keep programs and systems from realizing ideal interdisciplinary functioning. "As an administrator, I can say: as much as I believe in it, on a day-to-day basis it's very hard. When I say: 'How does this feel to you? What do you want to do?' I frequently get answers I don't want to hear, things that will make my job harder."

Personalities and professional hierarchies can create an imbalance in influences on decision-making. A psychologist says: "The most significant variable is the individual personalities in the group, their ability to control other people. It's not necessarily the discipline or the child's problems that create this influence. A lot of people don't want to admit that." Within the professional hierarchy it is often the physician who will claim the authoritarian role. "With the physician we had in our group, it frequently came down to: 'I am the physician. I direct this clinic and this is what we will do,' " says one practitioner. "We would often say yes and then go ahead and do things our own way anyway, but it was silly." Similarly, school principals or program directors are also in a position to make such authoritarian decisions.

When interdisciplinary teams are mandated, their makeup can be defined administratively, for convenience and to save money. "I know there have been plans developed for children that involved a school administrator, school nurse, and school psychologist," says a therapist. "These are decisions being made about disabled children without a therapist even present. There are a lot of people making decisions for these children who aren't even in the discipline for which they are suggesting recommendations. I find this really frustrating."

Decision-making processes can be improved. One way to do this is with experience and time. Teams and agencies within a community who work with each other have the opportunity to develop trust and to gain experience with what works best. The limitations are that it takes a long time, and that in some constellations of individuals, it may never work at all.

Training, either preservice or inservice, can offer pictures of what quality interdisciplinary decision making is really like and can present the techniques to accomplish it. Structure in the program itself, that is, specifications for the way meetings are run, for the assignment of leadership roles and for the clarification of expectations, is also important. There also has to be some pressure to promote good interdisciplinary decision making. An administrator offers one example: "We contract with physicians for service on our team. When I interview I make the expectations clear, for example, that the job includes attendance at weekly staff meetings, and I describe the philosophy behind those meetings. It isn't the whole answer, but it's a start."

## INDIVIDUALS AS SOURCES OF SERVICE SYSTEM CHANGE

For most parents of at-risk and disabled children, it is individual professionals who make or break a program. A professional's sensitivity, ability to identify with the problems of the family, and confidence to share information in a nonthreatening way, are the indicators of good professional-family relationships. These same personal abilities can contribute to the building of community and statewide programs. Legislation and funding alone do not determine the quality of services: people do.

The history of the development of early intervention services shows that a few people with vision do make a difference. It has not been a widespread public belief in early intervention that has led to the establishment of effective programs, but the ongoing investment of time by a few committed people, such as parents, legislators, school administrators, teachers, social workers, and nurses, who have talked, pushed, cajoled, and dragged such programs into existence.

Similarly, it is not only individual efforts of leadership that determine effective service structure. Most practitioners will attribute the best aspects of their programs not to administrative edicts but to the ways that people have learned or are learning to function together. When an individual family presents a complex problem for service coordination, regardless of the mandates of PL 99-457, there will always be a plausible excuse for why things can't be done. For example, a therapist, uncomfortable working with a medically fragile young child, can throw up her hands in frustration because the education system for which she works has no formal working relationship with health care settings. Or, she can find a visiting nurse who has contact with the family and form her own mini-system of coordination around this child. As the nurse and therapist develop an informal working relationship for children of joint concern, this personal system can influence the agency system.

While "system" barriers to best practices are often real, parents and professionals can learn to challenge or work around them. We expect a great deal from parents in terms of their abilities to change the system, and they often provide models for what is really possible. "Gina was in one program for 8 months but we needed something that could adapt to my work schedule," says a mother who is a professional in public relations. "So I talked someone into creating one. A friend and I were in the same boat with our kids, so we went to someone we knew . . . it took about 6 months. I guess it's like anything else: it's presenting the facts that there's a market and talking someone into doing it."

People who urgently sense the needs of young at-risk and disabled children may find it difficult to concentrate on small gains in the system when they have a working vision of the way the system as a whole should change for the benefit of children and families. While it is a giant step forward, PL 99-457 will not cure this frustration. Early intervention services clearly need both kinds of efforts: efforts to change the system through legislation and regulatory mechanisms, and individualized efforts that demonstrate that a changed system can be better.

## SUMMARY

In this chapter, we outline the elements of service that need to be in place, some factors that influence how these elements will function, and some organizational themes regarding what makes service elements work together effectively. These themes are as follows:

1.  National or state mandates for services should promote the definition of service needs, not the exact agency structures or methods by which the needs will be met. The organization of services is best planned from the delivery level up, not from regulations down.
2.  "Good" interdisciplinary strategies are not untried ideas, but strategies that have actually worked; good policy builds from good history.
3.  Service delivery plans must be built around manageable geographic areas, and upon the strengths of existing patterns of interagency function and communication.
4.  Service delivery planning should be concerned with decision-making processes, and with how to get all involved parties working with each other.
5.  Service coordination potentially represents a more serious barrier to effective delivery of services than funding levels.
6.  Determining access to programs and coordinating services are controversial processes in the organization of services.

Carrying out these processes in ways that are acceptable to all concerned will positively influence service delivery for individual families and children.

7. Legislation does not determine the quality of service delivery: people do. The history of early intervention services shows that a few people with vision do make a difference.

8. Individual practitioners are in a position to bring services more in line with best practices, despite administrative and policy barriers. Effective practitioners work on improvements to areas of the system with "give," rather than assuming that nothing can be done until system changes are mandated from above.

9. People who urgently sense the needs of at-risk and disabled children may find it difficult to concentrate on small, permanent changes in the service system when they have a working vision of the way the system *as a whole* should change for the benefit of children and families.

The elements of personal effort that we have attempted to emphasize in this chapter are not substitutes for change in the system. They are part of the process of creating change while delivering, and learning how to better deliver, services that address the long-term needs of at-risk and disabled children and their families. In the face of current barriers in the system, what can be done to improve services? Interdisciplinary answers to this question will point to the kinds of programs that can provide individualized support and resources, and that will allow for the individual strengths and commitments of practitioners to flourish.

In Chapter 7, issues related to PL 99-457 are summarized, and steps for starting new programs, or for improving existing ones, are offered.

# Chapter 7

# The Public Law/
# Action Steps

P ublic Law 99-457 declares a national interest in using early intervention services: 1) to enhance the development of handicapped infants and toddlers and minimize their potential for developmental delay, 2) to reduce special education costs by reducing the number of children who will need it, 3) to maximize the potential for eventual independence of handicapped children, and 4) to enhance the capacity of families to meet the special needs of their handicapped children. To act upon this national interest, the federal government will: 1) provide financial assistance to states to implement statewide early intervention services, 2) coordinate payment for those services, and 3) enhance the states' capacity to provide quality early intervention services and to expand and improve existing services.

## PUBLIC LAW 99-457

PL 99-457 calls for a *system*, not an exploratory piece of the puzzle. The fourteen minimal requirements will present significant challenges even to those states with more advanced services. For those with less developed resources and more limited finances, phasing in services will be complex.

During the development of the first edition of this manuscript several years ago, we felt honored to have the participation of national figures in the area of early intervention and of committed and articulate "grassroots" parents and service providers. Some of the individuals who helped us then were participants in the development and passage of PL 99-457.

It is clear that PL 99-457 considers many of the ideas central to quality early intervention. The emphasis on nurturing the family as part of enhancing the child's development, on personnel training, and on interagency collaboration are clearly reflective of the best thinking in the area. The opportunity is here now to carry out these ideas for the benefit of children and families. In this last chapter, we summarize some of the issues surrounding the law itself that will be part of this effort; in addition, suggestions for translating the law's important principles into practice are provided.

### The Limits of the Law

*Public Law 99-457 is the Beginning of a Process*   Given the sweeping and complex nature of PL 99-457, it will be important to see this legislation as a growing thing, not a static edict with permanent weaknesses. After close to 15 years, PL 94-142 is still evolving, and it must still be clarified and reinterpreted. There is every reason to believe that this will also happen with PL 99-457. Therefore, it is important to begin implementation and to reinterpret problem areas as they emerge.

*There Will Always Be Conflict between the "System" and the Intimate Service of Early Intervention*   Early intervention as a service takes place in the relationship and interactions between families, children, and professionals. At its best, it is an intimate and individualized effort. As has already been pointed out, the concept of flexible, individualized family "centeredness" is an inconvenient concept from an administrative viewpoint. As the system emerges, there will be an ongoing philosophical tug-of-war between the need for efficient administration and the need for creative and flexible responses by direct-care personnel to the changing and sometimes chaotic nature of families and children in need. The collective wisdom used in planning this system will determine where the balance will rest.

*The New Law Will Not Provide Everything that Families*

*Need* The greatest fear that many practitioners have is that the law seems to promise a system to make the family the ideal, strong, and wholesome environment needed by the child with disabilities. Direct-care staff are therefore concerned about the scope of the IFSP and whether they will be expected to function as marriage and family counselors, or to fill other roles for which they are ill-prepared. Defining the parameters of this mandate will be another area of balance that states must achieve.

*Early Intervention Is Still in the Process of Defining Itself* While the law clearly articulates a faith that early intervention will accomplish such things as increased independence, stronger families, and a decreased need for special education services for the child upon reaching school age, research has provided uneven answers to the questions of what kind of services can accomplish these goals. It will be important to maintain the scientific mode as these state systems emerge. A perception of unkept promises could set the scene for a backlash.

*The Law Cannot by Itself Carry Out a Revolution in Service Practices* The concepts of meaningful collaboration between families and professionals, and of true family centeredness in services are still, in practice, revolutionary concepts. There is a world of difference between talking about parent empowerment and making it a reality. The barriers that have existed to this shift from talk to practice will not be overcome by the law alone. To make the most important parts of this law a reality, it will take creativity and vision, as well as the continued vigilance of parents and other advocates who have been so central to the establishment of these principles.

## The Basic System Questions

As people begin implementation work, it will be important to maintain the overview both of the goals of the law and of how they are meant to be carried out. After establishing the goal regarding the need for state systems of early intervention, the legislation outlines 14 basic requirements. States must develop and identify the following:

1. A definition of developmental delay
2. A timetable for availability of services

3. A comprehensive multidisciplinary evaluation of the needs of children and families
4. An individualized family service plan that includes case management services
5. A child find and referral system
6. A public awareness program to focus on early identification
7. A central directory of services, resources, state experts, research, and demonstration projects
8. A comprehensive system of personnel development
9. A single line of authority to a lead agency
10. A policy for contracting or making arrangements with local service providers
11. A procedure for timely reimbursement of funds
12. Procedural safeguards
13. Policies and procedures for personnel standards
14. A system for compiling data regarding the early intervention programs

These requirements are meant to organize the states' answers to the following seven basic questions.

*What Children Will Our State Serve through This Early Intervention System?* The first requirement is that states develop a definition of developmental delay (Requirement 1) that will define which children will be served. In addition, the states must decide whether they will include at-risk children in their service criteria.

*How Will These Children and Their Families Be Brought into Contact with Services?* Here the law requires a system of child find for the state (Requirement 5). In addition, public awareness efforts are mandated (Requirement 6), so that the benefits and resources available through this system will be known.

*What Strengths and Needs Do These Families and Children Have?* The evaluation component (Requirement 3) called for in the law and the IFSP (Requirement 4) are meant to identify the strengths and needs of children and families.

*How Will These Needs Be Met?* Various components of

the law call for identifying service needs and making those services available. The IFSP (Requirement 4) will specify the services that families could use to meet needs. A statewide directory of resources (Requirement 7) will make known the services that are available. Additionally, there is a timetable for making new services available (Requirement 2). Also, there is a mandate for a process to contract with service providers (Requirement 10), for pooling resources to fund those services, and for ensuring timely reimbursement for services (Requirement 11).

*What Kinds of Professionals Can Carry Out Early Intervention Services in Line with the Law's Mission of Family Support?* To get states to answer this question, the law calls for the development of personnel standards (Requirement 13).

*How Will These Professionals Be Trained and How Many Will Be Needed?* Here the law calls for a state plan for personnel development (Requirement 8).

*How Will We Know Whether the Intended Goal Is Being Accomplished and Whether the System Is Adequately Meeting the Needs of Children and Families?* Here the law calls for accountability through a lead agency (Requirement 9). It calls for due process for individual families and children receiving services (Requirement 12), and it calls for a statewide data collection process. Over time, this process will allow states to assess the effectiveness of services and will permit them to share this information on a national basis (Requirement 14).

## ACTION STEPS FOR
## IMPLEMENTING EARLY INTERVENTION SERVICES

It will not be easy to answer these questions in ways that will promote flexible collaborative interactions between professionals, families, and children. We have outlined some action steps that we feel can help implement the central features we have covered in this book.

Some of these steps are of importance at all levels of the implementation process, from individuals, parents, and practitioners at the community level to members of the state interagency coordinating councils. Mission statements, for example, are critical. Individuals and groups need to clearly articulate what it is they are taking part in. Individual program administrators and practitioners need to pay close attention to areas such as practices and efficacy and how to make parent-professional collaborations meaningful. At whatever level individuals are working in the implementation process, it is essential to keep as a "test pattern" specific interactions between the parent and practitioner, and to measure all decisions in terms of their effects on those interactions. In addition, we feel it is essential that parents and grassroots practitioners who participate in those interactions are brought, in meaningful ways, into decision making that affects the implementation process. The wisdom needed to answer these questions appropriately may be developed most fully in those people who are engaged in those relationships every day.

## MISSION STATEMENTS

Participants in implementing services should have a mission statement that may include:

1. A statement of philosophy and rationale for services
2. A statement of how family support will be defined and integrated with child development concerns
3. A statement that clarifies the goal of parent-professional partnerships
4. A statement of assumptions about the development of at-risk and disabled young children, to guide practices
5. A description of the structure and process to be used to include all partners needed for quality decision making

## PRACTICES AND EFFICACY

Participants in implementing services should have functioning policies in place regarding program practices and efficacy that include:

1. Written goals for the program and specified means of measuring family and child outcomes that are consistent with program philosophy and mission

2. A means of individually mapping child and family strengths and needs
3. A process for developing goals for individual children and families that maximizes parent decision making
4. A description of how family support efforts will be carried out in conjunction with developmental services for children
5. Specified methods for assessing and strengthening individual parent-child relationships
6. Methods for keeping discussions, assessments, and activities tied to observable behaviors in the child and caregivers
7. Assessment protocols that include recording observations of the child's spontaneous and adaptive responses and of interactive behaviors
8. Translation, through parent-staff discussions or documentation, of observations into ideas, not only about the child's development and potential, but also of ideas about the child's temperament, and ways in which the parent-child relationship might be supported
9. Procedures for carrying out interdisciplinary decision making and practices, including a description of:
   a. How goals will be established and reviewed
   b. How staff conflicts will be resolved
   c. How the interdisciplinary process will be promoted and monitored in decision-making processes
   d. How parents will be made partners on the interdisciplinary team
   e. How conflicts between staff and families will be resolved
10. A plan for ensuring that early intervention efforts are conducted in an investigative mode, including:
    a. Methods for collecting both quantitative and qualitative information about children and families
    b. Procedures for using this data in the assessment and alteration of program practices
    c. Communication channels for sharing program data with other programs on both a local and a national level

## PARENT-PROFESSIONAL PARTNERSHIPS

Participants in implementing services should have:

1. A plan for operationalizing parent-professional collaboration to be shared with all staff, parents, and caregivers involved in services
2. A referral and support relationship with existing parent-to-parent groups, or involvement in helping to create such support
3. The inclusion of parent-professional issues in the regular working discussions of interdisciplinary teams
4. An acknowledgment of the importance of parents as team members. This should be translated into:
   a. Measures of program efficacy
   b. Assessment of staff effectiveness
   c. Allocation of staff time and resources
5. A plan for monitoring and evaluating the status of parent-professional interactions, especially relating to procedures for decision making and times of transition or other times of stress for families

## SERVICE ORGANIZATION

Participants in implementing services should have policies regarding service organization that include:

1. A written description of how children gain access to needed services
2. A description of how the service coordinator will be identified in the IFSP, specifying the role of parents in this discussion
3. A plan for coordinating special health care services with other early services
4. An assessment of the interagency collaboration environment and how it can be improved
5. A system for monitoring staff efforts in interagency coordination, and for seeing that these issues are included in staff discussions

## SERVICE PROMOTION

Participants in implementing services should promote early intervention services by having:

1. A method for keeping data and "case studies" on program efficacy in a form that is understandable to nonprofessionals
2. Relationships with advocacy groups and other agencies and organizations so that shared concerns can be presented most strongly to policy makers
3. A plan for communicating with community pediatricians and other physicians as essential and powerful allies in promoting awareness of and involvement in early intervention programs
4. A system for disseminating information about the program (e.g., needs met, success stories) to key decision makers, such as legislators and service groups, as well as to local and state media

## PARENT AND STAFF TRAINING

Participants in implementing services should have a plan for formal and informal parent and staff training that includes such topics as:

Program services:

1. Strategies and techniques for improving observational skills
2. Strategies and techniques for improving team decision-making capacities
3. Strategies for improving communication and interviewing skills
4. Strategies for identifying parent-child interactions that are weak or faltering from those that fall within the wide range of normal
5. Cultural and individual variations in parenting that will affect assessments of parent-child relationships
6. Behavioral patterns—including temperament and interactive abilities—of children with varying types of disabilities, and the special risks these patterns can present to developing parent-child relationships

7. New research on child development related to early intervention efforts
8. New evaluation instruments and new strategies for using traditional evaluation instruments
9. Models of team interaction
10. Ways traditional curriculums can be adapted for individualized and dynamic programming that consider both process and content

Parent-professional relations:

1. Special training for parents in areas that will help them be effective team members, such as case management, advocacy, and communication
2. Understanding, encouraging, and working with parent-identified goals for the child and family
3. Communicating disciplinary information in understandable ways
4. Making community programs and information resources available to parents
5. Acknowledging that staff bring their own values, beliefs, and priorities to parent-professional interactions and that these staff-held values influence their "professional" judgment
6. Recognizing and accepting the diversity in all families, that is, the differences in values, beliefs, priorities, and aspirations

Service coordination:

1. Developing skills in understanding and providing case management services
2. Educating staff about other community services, including joint efforts with other programs
3. Learning about models of other community or state programs and about activities for coordinating services and improving interagency communication

Our hope is that this final chapter will be used as any developmental checklist should be used: with flexibility and respect for individual and group differences. What are we doing as participants in this system and is it what we really should be doing? Where are the areas of needed change? How can change be accomplished?

Public Law 99-457 is a commitment to provide families with the support needed to encourage the development of especially vulnerable young children. This is not a new commitment, but it is one that has been significantly strengthened and renewed by this legislation. It is in the spirit of renewal that the significant challenges ahead should be met.

# University of Iowa Birth-to-Three Project
## Categorized Annotated Bibliography

---

Categories:

- A. Child Development and Research
- B. Social Support
- C. Parent/Family Focus (needs, involvement, education)
- D. Neonatal Issues, Intervention, Follow-Up
- E. Identification, Assessment, Intervention
- F. Early Intervention Efficacy (outcomes, reviews, commentaries)
- G. Parent Authors
- H. Policy
- I. Other

## A. CHILD DEVELOPMENT AND RESEARCH

Ainsworth, M.D.S., Blehar, M.C., Waters, E., & Wall, S. (1978). *Patterns of attachment: A psychological study of the strange situation*. Hillsdale, NJ: Lawrence Erlbaum Associates.

Book about infant-mother attachment based on information from a standard laboratory procedure (the "strange situation") used to study patterns of infant behavior. The strange-situation procedure is explained, and the theoretical background of the research is presented. Study methods are described, and the authors' results are discussed as are comparable findings of other investigations. Individual differences in patterns of attachment are interpreted and their likely influence on development is considered.

Belsky, J. (Ed.). (1982). *In the beginning: Readings on infancy.* New York: Columbia University Press.

Collection of articles concerned with development in the first stage of life. Included, among others topics, are discussions of: the transactional model of development; continuity in development; parent-to-infant attachment; research involving infant perception and cognition; early stimulation and its effects on infant development; the mother, father, and infant as an interactive system; and the effect of day care on the cognitive, emotional, and social development of the child.

Belsky, J., & Tolan, W.J. (1981). Infants as producers of their own development: An ecological analysis. In R.M. Lerner & N.A. Busch-Rossnagel (Eds.), *Individuals as producers of their development: A life-span perspective* (pp. 87–116). San Diego: Academic Press.

Essay concerning the infant as an active contributor to his development. Pre- and post-natal factors affecting the family system, and subsequent parental behavior, are discussed. Topics include: the parents' individual development; quality of the marital relationship; and the community, cultural, historical, and evolutionary context in which the family exists. The authors examine how infants can influence these factors, thereby affecting their own development.

Blacher, J. (1984). Attachment and severely handicapped children: Implications for intervention. *Journal of Developmental and Behavioral Pediatrics, 5*(4), 178–183.

Overview of attachment in developmentally disabled children. Topics reviewed include: attachment assessment procedures; attachment studies with severely handicapped children; and preliminary findings from a study on attachment in severely handicapped children; and implications of these data for pediatric practice and intervention with parents and severely impaired children.

Blacher, J., & Meyers, C.E. (1983). A review of attachment formation and disorder of handicapped children. *American Journal of Mental Health, 87,* 359–371.

Review of research on attachment in handicapped children. Literature regarding attachment in general is examined, as are procedures used to assess attachment. Studies are reviewed that deal with attachment behavior of specific groups of handicapped children and special procedures used. The authors discuss other issues of attachment related to handicapped children, including developmental aspects of attachment, implications for out-of-home placements, and concerns related to child abuse.

Bloom, K. (Ed.). (1981). *Prospective issues in infancy research.* Hillsdale, NJ: Lawrence Erlbaum Associates.

Volume examining topics for infancy research. Topics include: characteristics of interdisciplinary research (Emde); the need for interdisciplinary perinatal research (Yogman); the many and varied responsibilities of primary care pediatricians (Keefer); a pediatrician's own interdisciplinary development (Brazelton); assessment of adult-infant interactional regulation—"synchrony" (Rosenfeld); the study of infant sleep-wake behaviors (Sostek and Anders); future issues in perceptual development (McCluskey) and social development (Papousek and Papousek).

Bower, T.G.R. (1977). *A primer on infant development.* New York: W.H. Freeman.

Book summarizing data about development during infancy. The author examines issues pertinent to the scientific study of infancy, describes learning abilities of the newborn, and considers the nature of infant smiling. Other topics discussed include early attachment behaviors; perceptual, motor, cognitive, and language development in infants; the effects of early experiences on later development.

Bretherton, I., & Waters, E. (Eds.). (1985). Growing points of attachment theory and research. *Monographs of the Society for Research in Child Development, 50* (1–2, Serial No. 209).

Monograph presenting a theoretical and methodological consideration of attachment theory as it relates to attachment across life span, attachment across generations, and attachment across cultures. The work is divided into four parts: retrospect and prospect of attachment theory; theory and assessment; adaptation, maladaptation, and intergenerational transmission; and cross-national studies of attachment in infancy. The central themes—that attachment is rooted in a behavioral-motivational control system and that individuals construct internal working models of self and attachment figures—are reflected throughout the book.

Call, J.D., Galenson, E., & Tyson, R.L. (Eds.). (1983). *Frontiers of infant psychiatry.* New York: Basic Books.

Compilation of papers (from the 1980 First World Congress on Infant Psychiatry held in Portugal) reporting current research in normal and psychopathological development in infancy. Contributors, representing a wide range of disciplines, discuss various aspects of development and infant-caregiver interaction during the first 6 months of life; the developmental impact of social disturbances; physiological anomalies; and professional interventions in infant problems, as well as infant assessment. Papers focus on specific assessments.

Call, J.D., Galenson, E., & Tyson, R.L. (Eds.). (1984). *Frontiers of infant psychiatry* (Vol. 2). New York: Basic Books.

Compilation of papers from the 1983 Second World Congress on Infant Psychiatry held in Cannes, France, an extension of the first volume (from the 1980 First World Congress). The present volume contains more emphasis on the mother-infant relationship; types of psychopathology in infancy; early intervention and prevention of psychological disorders in infancy; and the role of infant caregivers such as fathers and grandparents.

Chess, S. (1983). Mothers are always the problem—or are they? Old wine in new bottles. *Pediatrics, 71,* 974–976.

Essay focusing on perceptions of early and revised views of mother-infant bonding. The notion is reviewed that benefits of mother-infant contact in the first hours after birth can never be retrieved if lost. A revised view is explained, which also finds immediate postpartum mother-infant contact to be desirable. When it can not occur, however, human adaptability provides "fail-safe" routes to attachment. The author comments on the effects that newer views might have on current practices and theory and on the understanding of attachment in later infancy.

Cohen, S.E., & Beckwith, L. (1979). Preterm infant interaction with the caregiver in the first year of life and competence at age two. *Child Development, 50,* 767–776.

Report of a study designed to explore the relation between interaction with the caregiver and competence in high-risk infants at two years. Fifty preterm infants were observed in their homes with a focus on caregiver-infant interactions (at the ages of 1, 3, and 8 months), and the authors conclude that it is possible to identify predictors of a preterm infant's later competence from social transactions in the first months of life.

Craig, S. (Director & Co-Producer), & Tallon, K. (Co-Producer). (1982). *Right from the start* [Videotape]. Chicago: Prime Time School Television.

Film concerning early parent-infant attachment. The interactive capabilities of newborns are demonstrated, and aspects of early relationships are explored. Also considered is society's influence on parent-infant bonding, and organizations that provide parental support are reviewed. Included is footage from bonding and attachment studies, including works of Harlow, Spitz and Bowlby, as well as Brazelton, Fraiberg, Kennell, Klaus, and Weissbourd.

Cranley, M.S. (1981). Roots of attachment: The relationship of parents with their unborn. In R.P. Lederman & B.S. Raff

(Eds.), *Perinatal parental behavior (Birth Defects: Original Article Series, 17* [6]) (pp. 59–83). New York: Alan R. Liss.

Reports from two studies examining attachment behaviors of parents with their unborn children. Mothers and fathers were studied and found to demonstrate attachment to their fetuses. The nature of their relationships and their association with several variables were also explored, and results are reported for each parent. Also included are proposals for future research.

Fitzgerald, H.E., Lester, B.M., & Yogman, M.W. (Eds.). (1982). *Theory and research in behavioral pediatrics* (Vol. 1). New York: Plenum.

First volume of a series devoted to theory and research in behavioral pediatrics. Focusing on human development during infancy, each chapter addresses a theoretical question in early development, reports research findings, and attempts to relate the studies to clinical practice. Topics covered include early intervention (Brazelton), a research instrument for the assessment of preterm infants' behavior—APIB (Als, Lester, Tronick, & Brazelton), crying (Lester & Zeskind), the role of physical appearance (Hildebrandt), and the father-infant relationship (Yogman). Also included is a manual for the APIB.

Fraiberg, S. (Ed.). (1980). *Clinical studies in infant mental health: The first year of life.* New York: Basic Books.

Collection of clinical case reports (from the Child Development Project, an infant mental health program at the University of Michigan) describing problems in the identification and treatment of infants at risk. The history, philosophy and structure of the program are described, as are selected case reports that illustrate its referral process, treatment methods, forms of intervention, and efforts to introduce infant mental health services to community health clinics. The clinical case reports, which comprise much of the volume, include descriptions of the persons and problems involved in each case, staff observations and suggested treatment methods, the results of periodic follow-ups, and an analysis of the program's handling of the case.

Garmezy, N., & Rutter, M. (Eds.). (1983). *Stress, coping and development in children.* New York: McGraw-Hill.

Volume exploring the effects of stress on children and ways in which they cope and adapt. Issues and perspectives include: children's stress due to the loss of a significant caregiver or due to the effects of war; neurochemical and physiological aspects of stress; significant stressors during the newborn period, infancy, early and middle childhood, and adolescence; the ecology of the family (when affected by divorce or a child with antisocial behavior) as a stress agent; the purpose of research on stress and coping, as well as its methodological problems and future directions.

Greenspan, S.I. (1981). *Clinical infant reports: No. 1. Psychopathology and adaptation in infancy and early childhood.* Madison, CT: International Universities Press.

Monograph applying a developmental structuralist approach to the diagnosis and treatment of psychopathology in infants and young children. The author describes six experiential organizations (structures) that correspond to six stages of emotional and cognitive experience during the first 4 years. For each stage, developmental capacities are discussed, as are environmental characteristics, common fears in the caretaker, and principles of preventive intervention and treatment. Clinical illustrations are also included to show the relationship between theory and practice. The appendix contains an outline of clinical landmarks for adaptive and disordered infants and early childhood functioning, based on a developmental structuralist approach.

Kagan, J. (1982). *Psychological research on the human infant: An evaluative summary.* New York: William T. Grant Foundation.

An appraisal of the state of research on the human infant. The author considers four categories in contemporary research: 1) cognitive development, 2) attachment, 3) psychological continuity, and 4) psychological consequences of prenatal and perinatal biological risk. Seven areas for future research are recommended.

Kagan, J. (1984). *The nature of the child.* New York: Basic Books.

Collection of essays presenting themes and critiquing assumptions about human development. The author emphasizes the influence of biological maturation on the development of cognitive abilities and readiness for processing of environmental experiences. He further interprets development in terms of both discontinuity and continuity and discusses his skepticism about strong connections between earlier and later development. Other themes and the author's perspectives, are presented in chapter-essays concerning the child's morality, emotions, and cognitive processes as well as the influence of the family on the child.

Kagan, J., Kearsley, R.B., & Zelazo, P.R. (1978). *Infancy: Its place in human development.* Cambridge, MA: Harvard University Press.

Presentation of results from an investigation on the effects of group care on the young child's psychological development. The authors review issues regarding the nature of early psychological development; infants and their development; and the effects of early experience on development. The investigation design, which focused on children from working- and middle-class families, involved comparisons of development between children who attended a day care program and children raised at home. The effects of group day care and the influence of ethnicity are examined, as are implications of the study's results. The appendix contains empirical data from the assessments used in the investigation.

Klaus, M.H., & Kennell, J.H. (1981). *Parent-infant bonding* (2nd ed.). St. Louis: C.V. Mosby.

Volume regarding the earliest parent-child relationship and factors that affect attachment. Subject areas include: family experiences during pregnancy; maternity practices during labor, birth and the early postnatal period, and their effect on bonding; needs of siblings; maternal behavior in mammals; and needs, concerns and practices to be considered in caring for parents of infants who are either premature or sick, have congenital malformations, or were stillborn or died in infancy.

Korner, A.F. (1983). Individual differences in neonatal activity: Implications for the origins of different coping styles. In J.D. Call, E. Galenson, & R.L. Tyson (Eds.), *Frontiers of infant psychiatry* (pp. 379–387). New York: Basic Books.

Report on a study of the quality, quantity, and style (over time) of neonatal activity and levels of energy expenditure. The study identifies measures of the infants' activity characteristics, and implications for neonatal activity research and for longitudinal studies of the origins of different coping styles are discussed. Also included is a review of literature that relates individual differences in activity and levels of energy expenditure to later personality characteristics and temperamental differences, and a brief description of a follow-up study relating early infancy data to later energy expenditure and temperamental differences.

Lamb, M.E., Thompson, R.A., Gardner, W., & Charnow, E. (1985). *Infant-mother attachment: The origins and developmental significance of individual differences in strange-situation behavior.* Hillsdale, NJ: Lawrence Erlbaum Associates.

Book presents and evaluates the literature dealing with the origins, interpretation, and developmental significance of individual differences in early infant-parent attachment, specifically with regard to strange situation behavior and the theory of attachment—two constructs which the authors feel must be distinguished more clearly. Theory and empirical research are reviewed. Evolutionary biology and developmental processes are discussed in an attempt to explore individual differences in socioemotional development. Aspects of the subject that are considered include:

background of strange situation research; interpreting strange situation behavior; stability and prediction; cross-national research; alternative analytic approaches; and future directions for research.

Lerner, R.M., & Busch-Rossnagel, N.A. (Eds.). (1981). *Individuals as producers of their development: A life-span perspective*. San Diego: Academic Press.

Volume exploring implications of the idea that individuals are producers of their development. This idea is analyzed within the context of infancy, childhood, adolescence and young adulthood, middle age, and the later years. Also examined are some variables that may provide a basis for a person's role in his own development. These include: temperament, the physical setting of development, physical disability, sex, race, and physical attractiveness. Contributors are from the fields of cultural anthropology, psychiatry, psychology and special education.

Lewis, M. (Ed.). (1983). *The origins of intelligence: Infancy and early childhood* (2nd ed.). New York: Plenum.

Collection of essays addressing issues in infant intelligence. Subjects covered: The relationship between sociopolitical views and the nature of intelligence; the history of infant intelligence tests and their value and limitations; perspectives on early mental development; a Piagetian view of the organization of intelligence; the existence of species-typical patterns and individual differences; the relationships between infant learning and intelligence, environmental risks and intelligence, social intelligence and communicative competence; effects of culture, social class, temperament, and affect on intelligence; theories about motivation and its relationship to cognition; and the nature of, and perspectives on, mental retardation in children.

Lewis, M., & Rosenblum, L.A. (Eds.). (1974). *The effect of the infant on its caregiver*. New York: John Wiley & Sons.

Initial volume of "The Origins of Behavior" series focusing on the effect infants have on their caregivers. Several chapters deal with various aspects of the infant-caregiver relationship, and results from research regarding the effect of several variables (such as size, shape, maturity, state, sex, sleep in premature infants, age and species) on caregiver response are considered. Also included are chapters on mother-infant interaction related to facial, vocal and gaze behaviors, and communication between blind infants and their mothers.

Lewis, M., & Taft, L.T. (Eds.). (1982). *Developmental disabilities: Theory, assessment and intervention.* New York: Spectrum Publications.

Volume comprised of presentations from a 1979 Chicago symposium entitled "Developmental Disabilities and the Preschool Child." Chapters focus on the study, assessment and treatment of developmentally disabled children in five areas of developmental functioning. These areas include: sensory development (primarily visual and auditory); motor development; cognitive development; language development; and the development of affect and temperament. Contributors include noted health professionals, educators, and developmental psychologists.

Lipsitt, L.P. (1978). Sensory and learning processes of newborns: Implications for behavioral disabilities. *Allied Health and Behavioral Sciences, 1,* 493–522.

Article reviewing implications of research on newborn neurological and behavioral capabilities for identifying and intervening with infants at risk for developmental disabilities. Research on sensory and learning processes of newborns is reviewed, and the author discusses how it has expanded knowledge about the relationship of early experiences to later development.

Lipsitt, L.P. (1981). Sensorimotor development: What infants do and how we think about what they do. In I.E. Sigel, D.M. Brodzinsky, & R.M. Golinkoff (Eds.), *New directions in Piagetian theory and practice* (pp. 29–37). Hillsdale, NJ: Lawrence Erlbaum Associates.

Discussion of the concept of stages in human development. Some shortcomings of the concept are detailed, and recent attempts to understand the mechanisms and processes of object permanence behavior (particularly Stage IV error in Piaget's theory) are reviewed. In summarizing such attempts, the author states that "the positing of hypothetical structures to account for behaviors which accrue and which are in continuous state of change is at best gratuitous, particularly when the structures are essentially response-defined rather than tied to specific antecedents or manipulable stimulation."

Lipsitt, L.P. (1982). Developmental jeopardy in the first year of life: Behavioral considerations. In A. Baum & J.E. Singer (Eds.), *Handbook of psychology and health* (Vol. 2, pp. 23–37). Hillsdale, NJ: Lawrence Erlbaum Associates.

Essay hypothesizing that the cause of certain crises in infancy may be related to sensory and behavioral processes. The behavioral repertoire of babies and the nature and functions of infancy are briefly reviewed, as are data from studies of sudden infant death and failure-to-thrive syndromes (SIDS and FTTS). Characteristics and processes common to both syndromes are examined. The author suggests that these crises may be partly attributable to infants' sensory and learning characteristics in combination with environmental conditions that affect learning experiences.

Lipsitt, L.P., & Reese, H.W. (1979). *Child development.* Glenview, IL: Scott, Foresman.

Book designed to serve as an introduction to child psychology. Selected topics include: the history, scope, and philosophical roots of child psychology as well as its methodology; contributions of heredity and environment to behavior and development; emotional, cognitive, and communication development; the role of punishment and adversity in development; and the place of scientific knowledge and objective methods in research.

Minifie, F.D., & Lloyd, L.L. (Eds.). (1978). *Communicative and cognitive abilities: Early behavioral assessment.* Baltimore: University Park Press.

Compilation of papers (from a 1978 conference cosponsored by the National Institute of Child Health and Human Development and the Child Development and Mental Retardation Center at the University of Washington) exploring relationships between communicative and cognitive development. Subjects include: cognitive, behavioral and sensory assessment; memory, sensorimotor and cognitive development; phonological development; language structure and pragmatic factors that influence language form; and the role of research in assessment and intervention with children having communicative or cognitive delays.

Murphy, L., & Moriarty, A. (1976). *Vulnerability, coping and growth: From infancy to adolescence.* New Haven: Yale University Press.

Volume reporting findings from a longitudinal study focusing on the ways children deal with stress and vulnerabilities using their own internal resources as well as those of the environment. Citing study data and also personal experiences described by the children, the authors review: aspects of the mother-infant relationships; processes that contribute to both continuity and change in coping; relationships between vulnerability, stress, and resilience; and children's ways of coping in the social and cultural context of the study's Kansas setting. Included in the appendices are data from the study, as well as information about measures, terms and approaches that were used.

Osofsky, J.D. (Ed.). (1979). *The handbook of infant development.* New York: John Wiley & Sons.

Compilation of works presenting new ideas, conceptualizations and research in the area of infancy. Topics covered include: various influences on infant behavior; early assessments; the differing perspectives of development; parent-infant and infant-infant relationships; continuity and change during development; and clinical issues, applications, and interventions. Most of the contributions to the volume are from noted authorities in the fields of psychology and pediatrics.

Osofsky, J.D. (Ed.). (1987). *The handbook of infant development* (2nd ed.). New York: John Wiley & Sons.

Second edition that includes new contributions by major researchers and teachers reflecting growth and change in the field of infancy during the last decade. The volume contains information on normal development in infancy as well as on development in risk groups, intervention, and applied aspects. Overview areas discussed are: developmental perspectives; social, emotional, and interactive perspectives; assessment, methodology, and analysis; risk factors, clinical approaches, and interventions; and current issues and perspectives. Within this framework, specific issues examined are: perceptual development, cross-modal representation, memory, developmental behavioral genetics, risk factors and preventive interventions, continuities and discontinuities, and infant mental health. International chapters are included.

*Right from the start* [Videotape]. See Craig, S. (Director & Co-Producer), & Tallon, K. (Co-Producer), 1982.

Sameroff, A.J. (1982). The environmental context of developmental disabilities. In D.D. Bricker (Ed.), *Intervention with at-risk and handicapped infants: From research to application* (pp. 141–152). Austin, TX: PRO-ED.

Discussion focusing on the importance of the environmental context in understanding and remediating developmental disabilities. Stressing the need for a transactional model to explain development, the author discusses self-righting tendencies (those from the child's side and those from the caregiver's side), emphasizing that how parents interpret their child's behavior affects the child's developmental outcome.

Sameroff, A.J., & Chandler, M.J. (1975). Reproductive risk and the continuum of caretaking casualty. In F.D. Horowitz

(Ed.), *Review of child development research* (Vol. 4, pp. 187–244). Chicago: University of Chicago Press.

Chapter analyzing factors which increase the risk of poor developmental outcomes of children. Research identifying such factors is reviewed, as is selected research regarding the developmental implications of early caretaking practices. Two sources of risk are identified from the reviews (the continuum of reproductive risk and the continuum of caretaking casualty). Three developmental models (main-effect, interactional, and transactional) are examined, and the authors conclude that the transactional model is necessary to understand the range of developmental outcomes described in the literature. Also considered are implications of the authors' analysis for the understanding of deviant development.

Schiefelbusch, R.L., & Bricker, D.D. (Eds.). (1981). *Early language: Acquisition and intervention.* Austin, TX: PRO-ED.

Sixth volume in the "Language Intervention Series" (comprising papers from a 1979 conference held in Sturbridge, Massachusetts) focusing on how infants learn functional language. Subject areas include: developmental processes and functions of infant language development; mother-child interaction; relationships between language development and cognitive ability; a basis for early intervention program design and evaluation; and issues and strategies in early language intervention.

Stern, D.N. (1977). *The first relationship: Mother and infant.* Cambridge, MA: Harvard University Press.

Book examining early social interaction. The author describes the caregiver's repertoire of facial, vocal, and other behaviors and the infant's repertoire of behavior and perceptual abilities. Research and theoretical frameworks regarding the influence of the mother's and infant's behaviors on the interactive process are discussed, as are the structure and goals of the process, as well as its significance for de-

velopment. Maladaptive patterns of caregiver-infant interaction are analyzed and their possible causes are considered.

Stone, N.W. (1979). Attachment in handicapped infant-family
systems. *Journal of the Division for Early Childhood, 1,*
28–32.

Article examining attachment behaviors of the handicapped
child and his family, and what they imply for intervention
strategies. The nature of animal and human attachment is
reviewed, as are maternal and infant attachment behaviors
involving nonhandicapped and handicapped infants. The
author observes that handicapped infants and toddlers in an
intervention program demonstrated different patterns of attachment behaviors than nonhandicapped infants. A list of
parent capabilities is presented which is based on observations of reciprocal behaviors of parents with their handicapped children.

Thoman, E.B. (Ed.). (1979). *Origins of the infant's social responsiveness.* Hillsdale, NJ: Lawrence Erlbaum Associates.

Compilation of presentations (from a Johnson & Johnson
Baby Products Company pediatric round table conference)
exploring primarily the infant's role in the mother-infant relationship during the first year. Among the topics included:
newborn auditory capacities and infant perception of contingency; intervention to "optimize" infant development;
newborn psychophysiological change; aspects of newborns'
system of adaptive responses; methods and directions for
studying mother-infant interaction; maternal deprivation;
strategies for studying behavioral development; individu-
ality and change in mother-infant interactions; and infants'
perception of timing (temporal aspects of social behaviors).
Also included is a commentary about current views on the
nature of infancy and directions for future study.

Thomas, A., & Chess, S. (1977). *Temperament and development.* New York: Brunner/Mazel.

Volume examining the interaction of temperament with individual abilities and environmental factors, and what that

interaction implies for the understanding of development. Temperament studies are reviewed, including their history, theoretical base and methodology, and the authors describe the nature and procedures of their own work: the New York Longitudinal Study. Chapters focus on the relationship of childhood temperament to such variables as behavior disorder, developmental deviations, parent-child interaction, interpersonal relations, school functioning, and health care practices. Characteristics of temperament are considered, including its measurement and rating; its origins; its consistency and inconsistency over time; and its presence in the older child and adult. Implications of the studies for the understanding of development are described, as are theoretical issues related to the concept of temperament.

Wachs, T.D., & Gruen, G.E. (1982). *Early experience and human development*. New York: Plenum.

Volume reviewing research on the influence of experiences (in the first 5 years) on later development. Subjects include: approaches used by researchers to study early experience; the relationship of the physical, social, and interpersonal environments to both intellectual and social development; the relationship between social and cognitive development; the pattern, direction and duration of early environmental experiences; and the implications of research on early experience for work with children.

Walker, J.A. (1982). See annotation in category I.

Waters, E., & Deane, K.E. (1982). Infant-mother attachment: Theories, models, recent data, and some tasks for comparative developmental analysis. In L.W. Hoffman, R. Gandelman, & H.R. Schiffman (Eds.), *Parenting: Its causes and consequences* (pp. 19–54). Hillsdale, NJ: Lawrence Erlbaum Associates.

Chapter examining the infant-mother bond. Three major perspectives from which infant-mother ties have been investigated are reviewed, and models of the infant-mother bond are outlined. Critiques of the attachment construct are summarized, and the authors identify five "tasks" which they feel deserve attention in future research on attachment.

## B. SOCIAL SUPPORT

Bush Center in Child Development and Social Policy. (1983). *Programs to strengthen families: A resource guide.* Chicago: Family Resource Coalition.

Resource guide (developed by the Family Resource Coalition and the Yale Bush Center in Child Development and Social Policy) describing various family support programs around the country. The guide is designed for those starting a program of family support, those concerned with policy and services for children and families, and those involved with program evaluation. Programs are divided into eight types which represent the diversity of family support programs, and within each type, exemplary programs represent a wide range of settings, locations, funding, service delivery, staffing, and kinds of families served. Included in the description of each program are recommendations regarding program development and maintenance as well as a list of available materials.

Chandler, L.K., Fowler, S.A., & Lubeck, R.C. (1986). See annotation in category C.

Cochran, M.M., & Brassard, J.A. (1979). Child development and personal social networks. *Child Development, 50,* 601–616.

Description of an effort to integrate knowledge about child development with knowledge about social networks of family members. The personal social network is defined and its influence on parents and children is discussed. The developing child is considered, and the impact of the parents' social network on children's cognitive and social development is examined. The authors introduce a conceptual model for analyzing relationships between personal social networks and the development of children, and they propose directions for future research.

Crnic, K.A., Greenberg, M.T., Ragozin, A.S., Robinson, N.M., & Basham, R.B. (1983). Effects of stress and social support on mothers and premature and full-term infants. *Child Development, 54,* 209–217.

Report from a study examining the effects of stress and social support on maternal attitudes and early mother-infant behavior. One-month postnatal interviews of mothers of premature and full-term infants were conducted to assess maternal life stress, social support, life satisfaction and satisfaction with parenting. Mother-infant behavioral interactions were observed at 4 months. Results reflect the significance of social support for parents, parent-child relationships, and early child development.

Dunst, C.J., & Trivette, C.M. (1985). *A guide to measures of social support and family behaviors.* Chapel Hill, NC: TADS, University of North Carolina. (ERIC Document Reproduction Service No. 267 558)

Listing of selected measures of social support and related measures of family behavior characteristics. Key terms are defined, and studies are briefly reviewed which suggest that social support affects outcomes. Included is a matrix of measurement instruments and the dimensions they assess, as well as a bibliographic guide to the instruments.

Mitchell, R.E., & Trickett, E.J. (1980). Task force report: Social networks as mediators of social support: An analysis of the effects and determinants of social networks. *Community Mental Health Journal, 16,* 27–44.

Overview of the current literature on social networks, emphasizing research linking social networks to individual psychological adaptation. Included is a review of social network concepts, and determinants of networks are analyzed, as are their varied effects. Also considered are implications of a social network orientation for community mental health policies and practices.

Pascoe, J.M., & Earp, J.A. (1984). The effect of mothers' social support and life changes on the stimulation of their children in the home. *American Journal of Public Health, 74,* 358–360.

Report concerning the relationship of mothers' life changes and social support to home stimulation of their children. Sixty-nine families of children who had been in a neonatal intensive care unit were evaluated in a 3-year follow-up. The study population is described, as is the follow-up protocol, which included measures of environmental stimulation, maternal social support, and life changes. Results showed the number of life changes reported by mothers to be unrelated to the amount of stimulation they provided their children. Mothers perceiving more social support in their lives provided a more stimulating home environment regardless of the number of life changes.

Shonkoff, J.P. (1984). Social support and the development of vulnerable children. *American Journal of Public Health, 74,* 310–312.

Editorial noting the potential positive impact of social support on the development of "high risk" children. Definitions of social networks and support systems are given and their relation to positive, health related outcomes is described. A discussion of early intervention for "high risk" children and families is included, and questions are posed concerning the role of social support in early intervention programming.

Trivette, C.M., Deal, A., & Dunst, C.J. (1986). Family needs, sources of support, and professional roles: Critical elements of family systems assessment and intervention. *Diagnostique, 11,* 246–267.

Describes the Family, Infant and Preschool Program (FIPP), a needs-based, social support approach to providing and mediating both child- and family-level resources and services. The strategy used by FIPP includes: specification of family needs; identifying sources of support and resources; and staff involvement in helping families assess resources from their support networks. The importance of family involvement in all aspects of intervention is underscored.

Weissbourd, B. (1983). The family support movement: Greater than the sum of its parts. *Zero to Three, IV* (1), 8–10.

Essay describing the diversity of family resource programs throughout the country. New dimensions among many family resource programs are explained, including the ecological perspective of services, emphasis on primary prevention, recognition of parents as developing persons, broader roles of staff, and new approaches to evaluation and research. The forms and settings of a variety of programs are noted, as are basic assumptions underlying the family resource movement. Using examples, the author defines what is meant by "family support."

Yogman, M.W., & Brazelton, T.B. (Eds.). (1986). *In support of families*. Cambridge, MA: Harvard University Press.

Compilation of papers (based on a 1984 conference on the family held at Harvard Medical School) which considers the family as part of its extended system and the individual as part of its family system in an effort to suggest how families can help their children handle the stresses of daily living. Topics discussed are: theoretical overview: stress and coping in the family system; forces within the family: new roles; forces outside the family: working and family life; special stresses: divorce, chronic illness, and teenage pregnancy; and policy implications: education and government guidelines. Contributors are experts from the fields of child development, pediatrics, education, child psychiatry, business, and social policy.

## C. PARENT/FAMILY FOCUS
(needs, involvement, education)

Abidin, R.R. (Ed.). (1980). *Parent education and intervention handbook*. Springfield, IL: Charles C Thomas.

Volume regarding the interface between the scientific and professional knowledge base and professional practices with parents. Basic issues are addressed in three sections and include: interaction between parents and children, and professional roles and guidelines for working with parents; knowledge and skills required of parent educators working with special populations of parents, and common problems encountered; and brief critical reviews of parent education materials and packaged programs.

Affleck, G., McGrade, B.J., McQueeney, M., & Allen, D. (1982). Promise of relationship-focused early intervention in developmental disabilities. *The Journal of Special Education, 16*, 413–430.

Article comparing two intervention approaches: one focusing on teaching parents therapeutic and/or curriculum-based procedures, another focusing on the development of adaptive parent-infant and parent-professional relationships. Both approaches are reviewed, critiqued and contrasted, and the authors cite several programs that exemplify a relationship-focused approach. Characteristics and preliminary findings from the authors' own program (the Family Consultation Project) are described, and implications of a relationship-focused model of intervention are discussed.

Bailey, D.B. (1987). Collaborative goal-setting with families: Resolving differences in values and priorities for services. *Topics in Early Childhood Special Education, 7*(2), 59–71.

Article examines the conflict in values that frequently occurs between families and early interventionists. Examples are offered to illustrate the difficulties encountered when value conflicts arise. Collaborative goal setting is presented as a method for avoiding conflict and therefore providing more effective early intervention.

Benson, H.A., & Turnbull, A.P. (1986). Approaching families from an individualized perspective. In R.H. Horner, L.H. Meyer, & H.D.B. Fredericks (Eds.), *Education of learners with severe handicaps: Exemplary service strategies* (pp. 127–157). Baltimore: Paul H. Brookes Publishing Co.

Chapter examines the changes in philosophy toward the role of parents involved in the care, education, and treatment of a family member with a severe handicap. The authors discuss the causes of the shifts in attitude, the ways such changes affect parents and other family members, and the current state of the art, as well as promising future directions in family involvement. Emphasis is on the concept of individualization. An assessment guide for a family systems approach is provided.

Bernheimer, L.P., Young, M.S., & Winton, P.J. (1983). Stress over time: Parents with young handicapped children. *Journal of Developmental and Behavioral Pediatrics, 4,* 177–181.

Report from an investigation that examined perspectives on stresses as perceived by parents of handicapped children when they sought information and services. Data collected from families with young children having mild to moderate handicaps were related to three periods: 1) initial diagnosis, 2) first efforts at seeking services, and 3) transition from infant to preschool programs. Factors that seemed to be associated with stress were considered, and parent-professional problems were identified. The authors discuss implications of these findings for professional training and practice.

Brazelton, T.B., & Vaughan, V.C. III (Eds.). (1979). *The family: Setting priorities.* New York: Science and Medicine Publishing.

Collection of presentations (from a 1978 conference) focusing on contemporary family conditions that endanger children, and the need for social changes in order to support families. A variety of issues are addressed, among them: social attitudes of and toward families; the impact of social and cultural status on families; health care systems, practices, and research that affect families; family relationships with other systems, such as social services, policy-making, education, work, media, and mental health; and public policy and research regarding the family.

Bristol, M.M., & Gallagher, J.J. (1982). A family focus for intervention. In C.T. Ramey & P.L. Trohanis (Eds.), *Finding and educating high-risk and handicapped infants* (pp. 137–161). Austin, TX: PRO-ED.

Essay exploring the conception that parents play central roles as educators and nurturers of their children and what this implies for intervention strategies. The movement toward a parent/professional partnership is briefly described, and factors involved in educating and raising children with handicaps in their home communities are discussed. Recommendations are offered for considering these factors in high-risk or handicapped infant programs.

Bromwich, R.M. (1981). See annotation in category E.

Bush Center in Child Development and Social Policy. (1983). See annotation in category B.

Carney, I.H. (1983). Services for families of severely handicapped preschool students: Assumptions and implications. *Journal of the Division for Early Childhood, 7,* 78–85.

Article describing guidelines for establishing partnerships between parents and professionals as they relate to services for children with severely handicapping conditions. Four assumptions concerning parent-professional relations are proposed, and their implications for practice are discussed. The author cites the needs of professionals and parents in developing partnerships and suggests areas for future research.

Chandler, L.K., Fowler, S.A., & Lubeck, R.C. (1986). Assessing family needs: The first step in providing family-focused intervention. *Diagnostique, 11,* 233–245.

Article examines the transition from child-centered to family-centered intervention strategies. Assessing family needs is seen as being crucial to long-term outcomes, social validity, and consumer support. Issues related to family assessment and suggested needs assessment are considered.

Clark, G.N., & Seifer, R. (1983). Facilitating mother-infant communication: A treatment model for high-risk and developmentally delayed infants. *Infant Mental Health Journal, 4* (2), 67–82.

Description of a mother-infant intervention program. The relationship between mother-infant interaction and the interactive communication process is examined with reference to high-risk and developmentally delayed infants. Intervention strategies are explained, and a hierarchy (range) of parental interaction behaviors is presented. Clinical examples illustrate parental behaviors.

Cochran, M.M., & Brassard, J.A. (1979). See annotation in category B.

*Equals in this partnership: Parents of disabled and at-risk infants and toddlers speak to professionals.* (1985). See annotation in category G.

Haskins, R., & Adams, D. (Eds.). (1983). See annotation in category H.

Hobbs, N., Dokecki, P.R., Hoover-Dempsey, K.V., Moroney, R.M., Shayne, M.W., & Weeks, K.H. (1984). See annotation in category H.

Joy, L.A., Davidson, S., Williams, T.M., & Painter, S.L. (1980). Parent education in the perinatal period: A critical review of the literature. In P.M. Taylor (Ed.), *Parent-infant relationships* (pp. 211–237). Orlando: Grune & Stratton.

Chapter describing types of currently available parent education programs and reviewing research on their effectiveness. The review is limited to programs that focus on teaching specific skills to parents and providing information about infant behavior in the perinatal period, with emphasis on programs that include formal evaluations. Implications for perinatal parent education are discussed.

Kirkpatrick, D.A., & Kirkpatrick, G.P. (1984). Principles of developmental pediatrics in private practice: They work. *Zero to Three, IV*(5), 5–8.

Description of the authors' pediatric practice in Chicago which focuses on preventive health care and early interaction with family and infant. A model for primary care is explained that includes a first neonatal visit in the hospital, a first office visit at three weeks, developmental screening and parent education by the third month, and continued contacts with the infant and family at 3-month intervals. Two case studies are presented that illustrate how the health care team works with infants who have developmental problems, and their families.

Klaus, M.H., & Kennell, J.H. (1981). See annotation in category A.

LaFarge, P. (1984). Mothers and pediatricians: Forming a team. *Zero to Three, IV*(5), 1–3.

A journalist's examination of mothers' attitudes toward their pediatricians. The author talked with mothers of various ages and income levels in parenting programs across the country. Included are the women's opinions about their relationship with their child's doctor; their doctor's authority, expertise, and personality; and their own role and authority in their child's health care. Barriers to mother-pediatrician relationships are also considered.

Laosa, L.M., & Sigel, I.E. (Eds.). (1983). *Families as learning environments for children*. New York: Plenum.

Volume regarding the family's influence on children's learning and development. Topics include: causal role of families in children's intellectual development; parents' teaching strategies; the development of literacy in children; families as social systems; and parent-infant play interactions. Also included are chapters on families with two wage earners, family day care, the beliefs held by family members about child behavior and development, and the development of household and social skills in children.

Lederman, R.P., & Raff, B.S. (Eds.). (1981). Perinatal parental behavior (*Birth Defects: Original Article Series, 17*[6]). New York: Alan R. Liss.

Compilation of research papers (from a 1980 conference in Ann Arbor, Michigan conducted by nurse researchers and funded by the March of Dimes Birth Defects Foundation) concerning the health and well-being of the family during the perinatal period. Subjects include, among others: the relationship of maternal prenatal development to progress in labor and fetal-newborn health; attachment behaviors of parents with their unborn child; correlates of parent-infant interaction; self-evaluated postpartum maternal adaptation; the relationship of maternal and infant variables to the maternal role in the first year; and the at-risk infant's impact on family relationships.

Lewis, M., & Rosenblum, L.A. (Eds.). (1974). See annotation in category A.

Mahan, C.S. (1981). Ways to strengthen the mother-infant bond. *Contemporary OB/GYN, 17,* 177–187.

Essay describing ways to foster mother-infant attachment. The importance of bonding is briefly reviewed, and the author points out several aspects of pregnancy that can affect mother-infant bonding. These include prepregnancy influences and planning, pregnancy and prenatal care, first visits to an obstetrician, parental reaction to fetal movement, and prenatal education. Labor and postpartum practices that encourage bonding are also discussed, as are ways to make the hospital more like a home environment.

McDonald, A.C., Carson, K.L., Palmer, D.J., & Slay, T. (1982). Physicians' diagnostic information to parents of handicapped neonates. *Mental Retardation, 20,* 12–14.

Report on a survey of physicians regarding their methods of providing parents with diagnostic information about their handicapped newborns. Sixty-nine Texas physicians were interviewed; questions pertained to the initial presentation of information to the parents, what type of information was provided, and what influenced the amount and type of information provided. The authors discuss the physicians' responses, particularly in reference to parents' perceived emotional and information needs.

McGillicuddy-DeLisi, A.V., & Sigel, I.E. (1982). Effects of the atypical child on the family. In L. Bond & J. Joffe (Eds.),

*Facilitating infant and early childhood development* (pp. 197–233). Hanover, NH: University of New England Press.

Review focusing on the relationship between the learning disabled child and parental beliefs and teaching practices. Research on parental beliefs about child development in the context of family variables is reviewed, as is a study that looks at the effects of parental beliefs and behaviors on the development of the learning disabled child with a language disorder. A case study is analyzed, and the authors discuss its implications for parent education.

McKay, S. (1983). *Assertive childbirth: The future parent's guide to a positive pregnancy.* Englewood Cliffs, NJ: Prentice-Hall.

Book designed to provide information so parents can make their own decisions regarding pregnancy, labor, and birth practices. The author explains how a support system can be built to provide for pregnancy and childbirth needs, and describes how parents can be assertive with health care providers. Medical controversies and changes are examined, as are pros and cons of current medications and medical procedures. Also included is a discussion of babies, their care, feeding, and possible problems, and an introduction to the Lamaze method of labor and prepared childbirth.

Mott, S.E., Fewell, R.R., Lewis, M., Meisels, S.J., Shonkoff, J.P., & Simeonsson, R.J. (1986). See annotation in category F.

Mulick, J.A., & Pueschel, S.M. (Eds.). (1983). *Parent-professional partnerships in developmental disability services.* Cambridge, MA: Academic Guild.

Volume (based on a 1981 Rhode Island symposium) dealing with relationships between parents and professionals in providing services for children with developmental disabilities. Chapters are grouped within four main sections: 1) professional counseling perspectives; 2) services and service providers; 3) family perspectives and community resources; and 4) societal perspectives. The fields of psychology, pediatrics, education, child development and social services are among those represented by the authors.

Pizzo, P. (1983). *Parent to parent: Working together for ourselves and our children*. Boston: Beacon Press.

Book examining self-help and advocacy among parents. Using interviews with members from national, state, and local parent organizations, the author focuses on the activities, problems and practices of parents in these groups, which include joint efforts to obtain better services for children, institutional reform, and mutual support among parents. The appendix contains an annotated listing of selected parent organizations.

Provence, S. (Ed.). (1983). *Clinical infant reports: No.2. Infants and parents*. Madison, CT: International Universities Press.

Collection of case studies illustrating diagnostic and therapeutic issues and methods in infant mental health services. Cases describe: a short-term, early intervention method by a pediatric multidisciplinary team; interventions involving infant-parent psychotherapy; assessment procedures and services of a mental health day care program; child and family assessment and treatment for severe developmental psychopathology; the child therapist's role; and an eclectic clinical approach to an infant and mother who presented multiple affective and developmental challenges.

Provence, S., & Naylor, A. (1983). *Working with disadvantaged parents and their children: Scientific and practice issues*. New Haven: Yale University Press.

Volume describing the Yale Child Welfare Research Program. The 1967–1972 program was designed primarily to help disadvantaged young parents encourage the development of their children and improve their family life. The program, its study population, staff, and services, are described. Its theoretical and clinical perspectives are discussed, and selected case reports are presented. A retrospective evaluation of the program's conceptual framework and effectiveness is also included.

Rosenberg, S.A., Robinson, C.C., & Beckman, P.J. (1986). See annotation in category D.

Shonkoff, J.P. (1983). See annotation in category I.

Smeriglio, V.L. (Ed.). (1981). *Newborns and parents: Parent-infant contact and newborn sensory stimulation.* Hillsdale, NJ: Lawrence Erlbaum Associates.

Volume (based on a conference sponsored by Johns Hopkins University and The Society for Research in Child Development) examining the experiences of newborns and parents in the hospital environment and their effects on infant development and parent-child relationships. Topics include: the effects of sensory stimulation in the neonatal period; research and issues involving early parent-infant contact, separation, and bonding; issues related to coordinating efforts of research groups; and suggestions for intervention research practices. Contributors include noted authorities in developmental psychology, nursing, pediatrics, public health, and sociology.

Stern, D.N. (1977). See annotation in category A.

Taylor, P.M. (Ed.). (1980). *Parent-infant relationships.* Orlando: Grune & Stratton.

Compilation of essays about the effects of perinatal care practices and attitudes on the quality of early parent-infant relationships and developmental outcomes of children. Chapter topics include: basic developmental processes in the parent-infant relationship (bonding and attachment, adaptation to pregnancy, newborn behavioral competence, emotional availability and rewards, the role of the father); effects of professional practices and educational programs; and approaches to intervention in relationships at risk.

Thornton, J., Berry, J., & Santo, J.D. (1984). Neonatal intensive care: The nurse's role in supporting the family. *Nursing Clinics of North America, 19,* 125–137.

Description of the intensive care nursery (ICN) nurse's role and functions in meeting family needs during infant hospitalization. Family responses to crises of newborns are discussed, as are specific considerations and methods that all ICN nurses can utilize in providing family support. The authors also describe how primary nursing, in particular, offers even greater support to families.

Turnbull, A.P., & Turnbull, H. R. (1986). *Families, professionals, and exceptionality.* Columbus, OH: Charles E. Merrill.

Volume considers the relationship among families, persons who are exceptional, and professionals and the ways in which they can work together more effectively. Topics covered include: historical and current roles of parents; family resources, interaction, functions, support, and life cycle; providing information to families; communication skills and strategies; the law of special education, due process, and the Education of the Handicapped Act; parent participation in developing the IEP; referral and evaluation; and professional ethics and morals. Appendices contain: a family assessment interview guide; a directory of parent information centers; a family information preference inventory; and the CEC Code of Ethics and Standards.

Vadasy, P.F., Fewell, R.R., Meyer, D.J., Schell, G., & Greenberg, M.T. (1984). Involved parents: Characteristics and resources of fathers and mothers of young handicapped children. *Journal of the Division for Early Childhood, 8,* 13–25.

Report about families participating in the Supporting Extended Family Members (SEFAM) program for fathers and their handicapped children. The SEFAM program is briefly described, and data are examined regarding the fathers' information needs and family responsibilities, both parents' levels of depression, demands on personal time, organized group affiliation, and satisfaction with present situations. Data gathered from fathers who participated in a pilot program were compared with data from fathers who had newly enrolled in the program. Responses were also obtained from the wives and compared with the fathers' responses. The authors discuss possible directions for study based on the SEFAM information.

Whitt, J.K., & Casey, P.H. (1982). The mother-infant relationship and infant development: The effect of pediatric intervention. *Child Development, 53,* 948–956.

Report from a study exploring the effects of a mother-infant intervention effort provided in conjunction with pediatric well-child visits during the infant's first six months. All participants received routine well-child care; control group mothers were engaged in discussions of physical and preventive care, and an intervention group was engaged in discussions about infant social development. At six months, infant and mother behaviors were assessed. The findings are presented with regard to: pediatric intervention effectiveness, infant development and the mother-infant relationship, and affective ratings and behavioral measures. Study results suggest that pediatric-based care can benefit the early mother-infant relationship. Directions for future research are considered.

Wiegerink, R., Hocutt, A., Posante-Loro, R., & Bristol, M.M. (1980). Parent involvement in early education programs for handicapped children. In J.J. Gallagher (Ed.), *New directions for exceptional children: No.1. Ecology of exceptional children* (pp. 67–85). San Francisco: Jossey-Bass.

Comprehensive review of what is known regarding parent involvement in early education programs. A history of parent involvement is presented including brief histories of Head Start, the Handicapped Children's Early Education Program (HCEEP), and PL 94-142. The role of parent involvement is examined, as is its influence on programs and projects, and a review of research on parent involvement examines its effect on both parents and the community. The authors conclude that parental involvement has been generally linked with positive child, parent, and program findings, but that the nature of the relationship is unknown (correlational versus causal). They further comment regarding the need to document and contrast different forms of parental involvement and their varied effects.

Yogman, M.W., & Brazelton, T.B. (Eds.). (1986). See annotation in category B.

Young, D. (1982). *Changing childbirth: Family birth in the hospital*. Rochester, NY: Childbirth Graphics Limited.

Reference text providing a comprehensive examination of family-centered maternity care. Topics include: principles and organization of some family-centered programs; needs and roles of family members and others; various environments and childbirth practices; roles, responsibilities, and practices of professionals; and care and services available to meet special family needs. Also included are chapters in which the author describes changes that are needed for increased family-centered maternity care, how these changes can be made, and how parents and professionals can be advocates for change.

Zeanah, C.H., & Jones, J.D. (1982). Maintaining the parent-staff alliance in an intensive care nursery. *Psychosomatics, 23,* 1238–1251.

Essay examining the relationship between parents and staff during newborn intensive care experiences, and the psychiatrist's role in monitoring the parent-staff alliance. Characteristics of a working alliance, including factors that hinder it, its impact on the parent-infant relationship, and healthy and weak alliances are described, as is the need for professional monitoring of the alliance. Problems for parents which threaten a healthy alliance are discussed, and three case studies illustrate psychiatric assessment and intervention.

## D. NEONATAL ISSUES, INTERVENTION, FOLLOW-UP

Brazelton, T.B. (1983). Assessment techniques for enhancing infant development. In J.D. Call, E. Galenson, & R.L. Tyson (Eds.), *Frontiers of infant psychiatry* (pp. 347–362). New York: Basic Books.

Examination of an infant assessment that considers examiners' subjective and clinical insights. The various uses of an assessment are discussed, with emphasis given to the benefits and procedures of the first evaluation of a neonate. Attempts by the author and others to develop and refine process-oriented assessment techniques are reviewed, and the continued work on a system to study each infant in depth in order to evaluate individual development is described.

Bromwich, R.M. (1977). Stimulation in the first year of life? A perspective on infant development. *Young Children, 32* (2), 71–82.

Review of research findings on aspects of neurological, affective, and cognitive development of infants and their implications for infant educational programs. The author suggests that the term "infant stimulation" is misleading and the concept associated with it questionable.

Cohen, S.E., & Beckwith, L. (1979). See annotation in category A.

Cohen, S.E., Sigman, M., Parmelee, A.H., & Beckwith, L. (1982). Perinatal risk and developmental outcome in preterm infants. *Seminars in Perinatology, 6,* 334–339.

Report of a study examining development, for the first 5 years, of preterm infants who suffered few or many neonatal complications. The study measured behavioral, neurological and physiological variables (using Obstetric, Postnatal, and Pediatric Complications Scales) and assessed caregiver-infant interaction (using naturalistic observations in the infant's home). Results suggested that "it is not possible to predict from most medical complications which infants will have developmental problems" and that "neonatal problems may have been ameliorated or increased by the caregiving environment." The authors conclude from the study that "the most important factor associated with developmental competence was responsive caregiving."

Escalona, S.K. (1982). Babies at double hazard: Early development of infants at biologic and social risk. *Pediatrics, 70,* 670–676.

Results from a portion of a study designed to examine interactions between biologic and social factors with regard to mental and psychosocial development of low-birth-weight infants. Development of premature infants, most of whom had significant illnesses and were from poor urban families, was followed for 3½ years. According to the author, results indicate that while cognitive and psychosocial development of both premature and full-term infants is impaired by environmental deficits and stresses, premature babies are the most vulnerable. The study's implications for pediatric practice and social policy are proposed.

Fewell, R.R., & Garwood, S.G. (Eds.). (1983). See annotation in category E.

Field, T.M. (Ed.). (1979). *Infants born at risk: Behavior and development*. New York: Spectrum Publications.

Volume presenting current research data on developmental follow-up of infants born at risk. Most of the studies are collaborations between developmental psychologists and physicians (obstetricians, neonatologists, pediatricians, and psychiatrists). Among the conditions studied are anoxia, low birth weight, prematurity, respiratory distress syndrome, metabolic disturbances, and central nervous system disorders. Relationships between perinatal complications and developmental outcome are discussed, as are the predictive value of early assessments and the development of infants born at risk versus infants not born at risk.

Field, T.M. (1983). High-risk infants "have less fun" during early interactions. *Topics in Early Childhood Special Education, 3*(1), 77–87.

Report from a study examining whether high-risk infants are less attentive and show less positive affective behavior and less frequent game playing than normal infants during early interactions. A group of normal infants and a group of infants considered at risk due to social unresponsiveness at birth, as well as their mothers, were studied for differences in attentive, affective, and game playing behaviors. The author concludes that the high-risk infants were less attentive, exhibited less frequent smiles and contented vocalizations, and cried and frowned more frequently than the term, normal infants. The author also describes interventions for adults which facilitate early interactions.

Field, T.M., & Sostek, A. (Eds.). (1983). *Infants born at risk: Physiological, perceptual and cognitive processes.* Orlando: Grune & Stratton.

Collection of research papers exploring processes that underlie behavior and development. Risk conditions studied include anoxia, low birth weight, prematurity, respiratory distress syndrome, bronchopulmonary dysplasia, and Down syndrome. Reports from three 5-year follow-up studies of infants are also included. Contributors to the volume include noted authorities from the fields of nursing, psychology, pediatrics, psychiatry, and child-family research.

Friedman, S.L., & Sigman, M. (Eds.). (1981). *Preterm birth and psychological development.* San Diego: Academic Press.

Volume reviewing psychological development in the preterm infant. Essay topics include, among others: sensory processing in preterm and full-term infants, parent-premature infant interactions, cognitive and visual development in preterm and full-term infants, the results of longitudinal follow-ups of preterm infants, biomedical and psychosocial interventions for preterm infants, and additional considerations for designing infant intervention programs. Contributors include noted authorities in child development, neonatology, pediatrics, psychiatry and psychology.

Gilderman, D., Taylor-Hershel, D., Prestridge, S., & Anderson, J. (Eds.). (1981). *The health care/education relationship: Services for infants with special needs and their families.* Chapel Hill, NC: TADS, University of North Carolina. (ERIC Document Reproduction Service No. ED 215 486)

Compilation of presentations (from a 1981 TADS/WESTAR conference held in New Orleans) addressing the need for building relationships between education and health care professionals. Some presentations are in abbreviated form and cover such topics as: the potential of neonatal assessment as an intervention; preterm and postterm assessments;

newborn and infant intervention strategies and program evaluation; parent and family involvement; and fiscal, legal, and ethical issues of neonatal care. Complete texts of speeches on the "building relationships" theme are also included.

Goldberg, S., & DiVitto, B.A. (1983). *Born too soon: Preterm birth and early development*. New York: W.H. Freeman.

Book about the development of preterm infants, written for parents and professionals. Special characteristics of preterm infants as well as their similarities to full-term infants are described, as are the neonatal intensive care unit environment and examples of intervention programs. Parents' experiences with their preterm infants are also included. The authors cite selected studies and discuss "average" preterm infant development.

Goldson, E. (1981). The family care center: Transitional care for the sick infant and his family. *Children Today, 10*(4), 15–20.

Description of a transitional nursery (The Family Care Center in the Department of Perinatology at the Children's Hospital in Denver) for infants recently moved out of neonatal intensive care. The goals, philosophy, environment, and structure of the center are discussed, as are its interdisciplinary approach to caretaking (involving physicians, nurses, occupational and physical therapists, child developmental specialists, and social workers) and its efforts to involve parents and siblings in the infant's care. Also described are the center's ongoing support system and developmental follow-up program.

Gorski, P.A., Davison, M.F., & Brazelton, T.B. (1979). Stages of behavioral organization in the high-risk neonate: Theoretical and clinical considerations. *Seminars in Perinatology, 3* 61–72.

Description of a model of neurobehavioral development for premature and sick infants. Theory and research regarding early neurological and behavioral development in high-risk neonates are presented, and the authors explain a three-stage model for such development in which parent participation is seen as critical to the infant outcomes. Clinical examples illustrate stages of the infant's physiologic organization, early behavioral responsiveness, and active reciprocity with the social environment. Clinical implications of the model are also discussed.

Juntti, M.J. (1982). Use of the Brazelton neonatal assessment scale to educate parents of high-risk infants. *Infant Mental Health Journal, 3,* 180–183.

Description of how the Brazelton assessment was used to help parents of high-risk infants recognize their babies' cues and capabilities. The rationale and methods of its use in this manner are discussed, accompanied by a clinical example of how the assessment process is explained to parents.

Kearsley, R.B., & Sigel, I.E. (Eds.). (1979). *Infants at risk: Assessment of cognitive functioning.* Hillsdale, NJ: Lawrence Erlbaum Associates.

Volume of selected papers (from a conference sponsored by The National Foundation-March of Dimes) examining what is currently known in the behavioral sciences about infancy and early cognitive development, and how this knowledge might improve the diagnosis and treatment of high-risk infants. Within this context, the chapters describe: Psychological processes (Lipsitt); visual cognition (Haith); perceptual-cognitive assessment (Zelazo); linguistic competence (Menyuk); variables related to later cognitive competence (Sameroff); the possibility that developmental retardation may result from incorrect placements and attitudes (Kearsley); alternative approaches to the current intellectual assessment of school-age mentally retarded children (Hamilton); and areas in intellectual development requiring continued exploration and additional research (Sigel).

Lederman, R.P., & Raff, B.S. (Eds.). (1981). See annotation in category C.

Mahan, C.S. (1981). See annotation in category C.

Mahan, C.K., Krueger, J.C., & Schreiner, R.L. (1982). The family and neonatal intensive care. *Social Work in Health Care,* 7(4), 67–78.

Essay examining topics regarding the needs and concerns of families of sick newborns. Parental responses to the birth of a sick infant are discussed, as are NICU practices that may aid parents; staff communication with the family; the role of siblings; and preparing the family for discharge. Also described are effects on family and staff of long term neonatal care; neonatal death; termination of life support systems; infants with handicaps; and the role of the social worker as part of the health care team.

McKay, S. (1983). See annotation in category C.

Meisels, S.J., Jones, S.N., & Stiefel, G.S. (1983). Neonatal intervention: Problem, purpose, and prospects. *Topics in Early Childhood Special Education,* 3(1), 1–13.

Review of studies regarding intervention with preterm infants and their implications for future research and practice. The authors report that such studies are confusing and inconclusive, lack comparability, and that their goals and objectives lack consensus. The authors contend that preterm infant development is enhanced by improving the conditions of infant-caregiver interaction and individualizing intervention efforts for infants and their families. A framework for neonatal intervention designed to encompass these considerations is presented, and the appendix contains sample developmental plans used by a hospital-based neonatal demonstration project and based on data from the APIB (Assessment of Preterm Infants' Behavior).

Nurcombe, B., Howell, D.C., Rauh, V.A., Teti, D.M., Ruoff, P., & Brennan, J. (1984). See annotation in category E.

Parmelee, A.H., Beckwith, L., Cohen, S.E., & Sigman, M. (1983). Social influences on infants at medical risk. In J.D. Call, E. Galenson, & R.L. Tyson (Eds.), *Frontiers of infant psychiatry* (pp. 247–255). New York: Basic Books.

Report of findings from a longitudinal study of infants at medical risk. The relationship between biological problems and environmental influences is considered with emphasis on both preterm and term infant-mother interactions. Differences between the two groups, individual differences within the term and preterm groups, and the influence of social factors on these interactions are also considered. The study's results are analyzed and their implications for intervention are discussed.

Rosenberg, S.A., Robinson, C.C., & Beckman, P.J. (1986). Measures of parent-infant interaction: An overview. *Topics in Early Childhood Special Education,* 6(2), 32–43.

Article considers the quality of parent-child interaction as an aspect of intervention. Types and styles of parental involvement with handicapped infants, and the advantages and disadvantages of each, are discussed. Suggestions for selecting appropriate tools to measure the effectiveness of parent-child interaction are also given.

Schaefer, M., Hatcher, R.P., & Barglow, P.D. (1980). Prematurity and infant stimulation: A review of research. *Child Psychiatry and Human Development,* 10, 199–212.

Review of stimulation literature related to premature infants. Studies that link prematurity with later developmental disability are examined, as are animal and human studies that have focused on stimulation enrichment or deprivation. The authors find that the evidence "strongly suggests that stimulation in infancy is beneficial, specifically for the premature infant," and implications of this conclusion for care of premature infants are discussed.

Sell, E. (Ed.). (1980). *Follow-up of the high risk newborn: A practical approach.* Springfield, IL: Charles C Thomas.

Collection of presentations (from a 1978 conference held in Tucson, Arizona) concerning follow-up care and programs for high-risk newborns. General subject areas addressed in the chapters include: morbidity and mortality; infant assessment and infant-caretaker interaction; specific medical conditions of high-risk infants; intervention programs for families with handicapped children; and parent involvement.

Smeriglio, V.L. (Ed.). (1981). See annotation in category C.

Tamir, D., Brazelton, T.B., & Russell, A. (Eds.). (1986). *Stimulation and intervention in infant development: Theories, evaluation and research, programs in the community, fetal behavior and intervention for the child at risk.* London: Freund.

Compilation of papers (from the 1984 First International Symposium on Intervention and Stimulation in Infant Development held in Jerusalem) reporting current understanding, research, and experience in the field of intervention as it relates to infants with normal development and to infants with developmental disabilities. Issues explored are: the basis of intervention in child development; intervention in the community; the child at risk; fetal development; and diagnosis and evaluation in child development. Contributors from around the world include experts in the fields of pediatrics, psychiatry, neurology, child psychology, social work, nursing, occupational therapy, and early childhood education.

Thornton, J., Berry, J., & Santo, J.D. (1984). See annotation in category C.

Waldstein, A., Gilderman, D., Taylor-Herschel, D., Prestridge, S., & Anderson, J. (Eds.). (1982). *Issues in neonatal care.* Chapel Hill, NC: TADS, University of North Carolina. (ERIC Document Reproduction Service No. 224 588)

Monograph focusing on the health care/education relationship regarding health services for infants with special needs and their families. Chapters address issues of assessment, intervention, and family support. Subjects include assessment as an intervention; use of the APIB (Assessment of Preterm Infants' Behavior) scale; the intensive care nursery environment, and the role of the developmental/educational specialist; the influence of a developmental consultation model on a care system for premature infants; the effects of hospitalization on siblings; issues regarding attachment; and effective communication and the professional role in family support.

Widmayer, S.M., & Field, T.M. (1980). Effects of Brazelton demonstrations on early interactions of preterm infants and their teenage mothers. *Infant Behavior and Development, 3, 79–89.*

Report from a study examining whether assessments of interactional skills of neonates might be used to enhance lower class teenage mothers' sensitivity to their infants' capabilities and thus encourage mother-infant interactions. One-month assessments were administered to mothers who observed the initial Brazelton demonstration of their infants and then independently administered the Mother's Assessment of the Behavior of Her Infant (MABI). The same assessment was done on mothers of preterm infants who only administered the MABI; these two groups showed more optimal interactions than two control groups. The authors found the combined Brazelton observations and independent MABI to be more effective than independent MABI use only, and they suggest that the benefits of the combined Brazelton/MABI intervention (for the first month of infancy) appear to exceed its minimal cost.

Young, D. (1982). See annotation in category C.

Zeanah, C.H., & Jones, J.D. (1982). See annotation in category C.

## E. IDENTIFICATION, ASSESSMENT, INTERVENTION

Affleck, G., McGrade, B.J., McQueeney, M., & Allen, D. (1982). See annotation in category C.

Blacher, J. (1984). See annotation in category A.

Blacher, J., & Meyers, C.E. (1983). See annotation in category A.

Brazelton, T.B. (1983). See annotation in category D.

Bricker, D.D. (Ed.). (1982). *Intervention with at-risk and handicapped infants: From research to application.* Austin, TX: PRO-ED.

Volume (from the 1980 Asilomar Conference entitled "Handicapped and At-Risk Infants: Research and Application") addressing the research-to-practice exchange. Among the topics covered are the role of theory in the study of handicapped and at-risk populations, the utility of available research literature, review of assessment issues and strategies, the environmental context in which assessment and intervention occur, the nature of selected social and developmental issues, and implications for intervention. Contributors are from various fields including psychology, education, occupational therapy, nursing, and pediatrics.

Bricker, D.D. (1986). *Early education of at-risk and handicapped infants, toddlers, and preschool children.* Glenview, IL: Scott, Foresman.

Handbook developed for early childhood special education students as well as for practicing professionals in the field. Designed to be an integrated text, part one examines key theoretical issues and foundations of intervention along with research findings on efficacy; part two explores practical applications of theory with an emphasis on program development and implementation. Appendices include: approximate age range for selected developmental skills; early-intervention programs; intake forms; and family impact measures.

Brinker, R.P., & Lewis, M. (1982). Discovering the competent handicapped infant: A process approach to assessment and intervention. *Topics in Early Childhood Special Education,* 2(2), 1–16.

Description of a process-oriented approach to assessment and intervention. The authors discuss the nature of "cooccurrences," the ability of infants to detect and utilize them, and the effect of the reduced cooccurrences (experienced by some handicapped infants) on parent-infant interaction. The authors propose a process approach to evaluation and intervention, and describe the Contingency Intervention Project, a curriculum (with microcomputer applications) designed to increase the infant's control of the environment and his awareness of contingencies.

Bromwich, R.M. (1977). See annotation in category D.

Bromwich, R.M. (1981). *Working with parents and infants: An interactional approach.* Austin, TX: PRO-ED.

Presentation of an approach to intervention that focuses primarily on the interaction between parent and infant. Using the UCLA Infant Studies Project Intervention Program as a model, the chapters focus on assessment and intervention by discussing specific cases, defining concepts and terms (including an explanation of the PBP [Parent Behavior Progression] assessment instrument), and citing problems in parenting and parent-infant interaction. Also included are the author's reflections on the intervention experience.

Brooks-Gunn, J., & Lewis, M. (1981). Assessing young handicapped children: Issues and solutions. *Journal of the Division for Early Childhood, 2,* 84–95.

Article addressing the need for effective identification, assessment and intervention, and importance of research in meeting these needs. The authors review problems related to current assessment techniques, as well as some possible solutions, and describe the Competency Assessment Project, which was designed to counter these problems. Data from the Project, and their implications for assessment, are examined.

Brooks-Gunn, J., & Lewis, M. (1983). Screening and diagnosing handicapped infants. *Topics in Early Childhood Special Education, 3*(1), 14–28.

Overview of issues in assessment of handicapped infants. Three levels of assessment: screening, diagnosis, and treatment, are considered, as are purposes, procedures, and selected tests for each level. Limitations of infant intelligence tests are reviewed. The authors discuss three areas of research that have implications for screening and diagnosing handicapped infants, and they also outline a focus for future assessment research.

Clark, G.N., & Seifer, R. (1983). See annotation in category C.

Dunst, C.J., & Gallagher, J.L. (1983). Piagetian approaches to infant assessment. *Topics in Early Childhood Special Education, 3*(1), 44–62.

Examination of the use of ordinal scales of infant development in infant assessment. The purposes and characteristics of ordinal scales are described, as are conceptual and pragmatic differences between ordinal and traditional psychometric infant scales. By citing clinical cases, the authors illustrate applications and uses of ordinal scales for assessment and intervention, including their usefulness in determining patterns of early cognitive development. Also examined are assessment strategies that utilize these patterns of development, the strategies' impact on assessment research, and limitations and cautions, as well as benefits, regarding the use of ordinal scales.

Dunst, C.J., Lesko, J.J., Holbert, K.A., Wilson, L.L., Sharpe, K.L., & Liles, R.F. (1987). A systematic approach to infant intervention. *Topics in Early Childhood Special Education, 7*(2), 19–37.

A systematic model for infant intervention with seven components is set forth. The goal of such intervention is to assist the child in developing conventualized competencies that demonstrate the child's ability to exercise control over the social and nonsocial environment through those competencies. The model is designed to provide a framework for those interventionists who are committed to assisting the child in achieving his or her own power base rather than promoting adult control and manipulation.

Fewell, R.R., & Garwood, S.G. (Eds.). (1983). Infants at risk. *Topics in Early Childhood Special Education, 3*(1).

Special issue on the high-risk infant. Included are articles on infant assessment (Fewell), neonatal intervention (Meisels, Jones, and Stiefel), infant screening and diagnosis (Brooks-

Gunn and Lewis), limitations of normative assessments (Shonkoff), Piagetian approaches to assessment (Dunst and Gallagher), communication between mothers and infants with Down syndrome (Mahoney), and mother-infant inter-actions (Field).

Fewell, R.R., & Sandall, S.R. (1986). A measurement dilemma. *Topics in Early Childhood Special Education, 6*(3), 86–99.

Article compares three standard research methodologies—developmental age, developmental quotient, and prediction indices—used to analyze data from a birth to three early intervention program. Problems in using these developmental scales are examined; inconsistencies in results are discussed. The importance of expanding assessment measures is stressed, and alternative directions for measurement of child progress are given.

Fitzgerald, H.E., Lester, B.M., & Yogman, M.W. (Eds.). (1982). See annotation in category A.

Garwood, S.G. (1982). (Mis)use of developmental scales in program evaluation. *Topics in Early Childhood Special Education, 1*(4), 61–70.

Essay proposing that the use of existing developmental scales for evaluating the effects of programs for handicapped children is inappropriate. A brief historical overview of the scales is given, and the problems associated with their use for special children are described. The author also offers several options for more appropriately determining the success of preschool intervention efforts for children with handicaps, including nonquantitative approaches.

Garwood, S.G., & Fewell, R.R. (Eds.). (1982). See annotation in category I.

Gilderman, D., Taylor-Herschel, D., Prestridge, S., & Anderson, J. (Eds.). (1981). See annotation in category D.

Guralnick, M.J., & Bennett, F.C. (Eds.). (1987). See annotation in category F.

Horowitz, F.D. (1982). Methods of assessment for high-risk and handicapped infants. In C.T. Ramey & P.L. Trohanis (Eds.),

*Finding and educating high-risk and handicapped infants* (pp. 101–118). Austin, TX: PRO-ED.

Overview of infant assessment methods. Included is a brief history of assessment, a discussion of why and how infants are assessed (prenatally, at birth, and neonatally), a review of assessment instruments, including those used in evaluating specific areas of competence, and a catalogue of checklists, profiles, and progress charts used to evaluate infants, plan intervention, and document progress.

Juntti, M.J. (1982). See annotation in category D.

Kearsley, R.B., & Sigel, I.E. (Eds.). (1979). See annotation in category D.

Lewis, M., & Taft, L.T. (Eds.). (1982). See annotation in category A.

Nurcombe, B., Howell, D.C., Rauh, V.A., Teti, D.M., Ruoff, P., & Brennan, J. (1984). An intervention program for mothers of low birth weight infants: Preliminary results. *Journal of the American Academy of Child Psychiatry, 23,* 319–325.

Report on the impact of the Mother Infant Transaction Program (MITP) on maternal and low birth weight infant outcome. The intervention program consisted of eleven sessions during which mothers were taught to identify and be more sensitive and responsive to their newborn infants' physiological and social signals. Six-month outcome measures of maternal adaptation and psychopathology, as well as infant cognitive development and temperament were analyzed, and impact of the program is discussed. The appendix contains an outline of the MITP.

Provence, S., & Solnit, A.J. (1981). Obstacles to early assessment and treatment of infants. *Children Today, 10*(4), 38–41.

Discussion of obstacles to early diagnosis and effective treatment of developmental and mental problems of infants. Principles that need to be observed in order for the obstacles to either be resolved or at least become less hindering are posited, and three case studies are examined which illustrate these issues and principles.

Ramey, C.T., & Trohanis, P.L. (Eds.). (1982). *Finding and educating high-risk and handicapped infants.* Austin, TX: PRO-ED.

Volume concerning the planning and operating of identification and intervention programs. Included are essays focusing on different aspects of such programs for high-risk and handicapped infants, including epidemiology, environments, methods of identification, screening programs, methods of assessment, and planning (and evaluation) of the programs. Also included are discussions on the family as a focus of intervention and on risk factors beyond the child and family. Selected demonstration programs for infant intervention are profiled, and annotated listings and questionnaires from screening and intervention programs are included. Contributors include Hayden, Horowitz, Bricker, Bristol, Gallagher, and the editors.

Sell, E. (Ed.). (1980). See annotation in category D.

Shonkoff, J.P. (1983). The limitations of normative assessments of high-risk infants. *Topics in Early Childhood Special Education, 3*(1), 29–43.

Overview of standardized tests in the assessment of infants and toddlers. Included is a history of intelligence tests with emphasis on the development of tests for the formal evaluation of infants; an examination of current priorities for early childhood testing and the historical and social contexts in which they were developed; a critical appraisal of normative tests used with high-risk children; and alternatives to traditional normative assessment. What the author refers to as the "current dilemma" of high-risk infant evaluation is summarized.

Simeonsson, R.J., Huntington, G.S., & Parse, S.A. (1980). Expanding the developmental assessment of young handicapped children. In J.J. Gallagher (Ed.), *New directions for exceptional children: No. 3. Young exceptional children* (pp. 51–74). San Francisco: Jossey-Bass.

Examination of issues regarding the valid assessment of severely handicapped children. Objectives for assessment are identified, as are problems involved in achieving them. The authors propose strategies with potential relevance for the assessment of severely handicapped children, and aspects of development are examined that need to be considered if such strategies are to be implemented. New directions based on these strategies are explored for clinical practice as well as research.

Stone, N.W. (1979). See annotation in category A.

Tamir, D., Brazelton, T.B., & Russell, A. (Eds.). (1986). See annotation in category D.

Taylor, P.M. (Ed.). (1980). See annotation in category C.

Uzgiris, I.C., & Hunt, J.M. (1975). *Assessment in infancy: Ordinal scales of psychological development.* Urbana: University of Illinois Press.

Text describing an approach to the assessment of infant psychological development that uses ordinal scales. The authors summarize past theories and concepts regarding development of intelligence and motivation and describe the six scales as well as the investigation from which they were derived. Also included are directions for using the scales.

Whitt, J.K., & Casey, P.H. (1982). See annotation in category C.

Widmayer, S.M., & Field, T.M. (1980). See annotation in category D.

Zelazo, P.R. (1982). Alternative assessment procedures for handicapped infants and toddlers: Theoretical and practical issues. In D.D. Bricker (Ed.), *Intervention with at-risk and handicapped infants: From research to application* (pp. 107–128). Austin, TX: PRO-ED.

Description of an information processing approach to the assessment of early development in children with developmental disabilities. Difficulties with conventional, standardized tests are discussed, as are assumptions related to such tests. Research on infant memory is reviewed and, based on this review, the assumption of sensorimotor intelligence is challenged. Perceptual-cognitive procedures, which assess information processing ability, are described as alternatives to conventional tests. The author cites a case study and preliminary results from a validation study that support an information processing approach.

Zelle, R.S., & Coyner, A.B. (1983). *Developmentally disabled infants and toddlers: Assessment and intervention*. Philadelphia: F.A. Davis.

Resource text integrating theory, research and personal experience into a working-level framework for clinicians involved in assessment and intervention of infants and toddlers with developmental disabilities. Chapters contain: a review of health care for handicapped infants; a framework for assessing normal developmental patterns, providing growth-fostering environments, assessing aberrant developmental and interactive patterns, and meeting habilitative needs during the first two years; approaches to elicit and interpret the attention level and response threshold in the infant or child; an approach to the assessment and habilitation of abnormal oral patterns; and a discussion about assessment and intervention of the preterm infant in the intensive care nursery.

## F. EARLY INTERVENTION EFFICACY
### (outcomes, reviews, commentaries)

Bailey, D.B., Jr., & Simeonsson, R.J. (1984). Critical issues underlying research and intervention with families of young handicapped children. *Journal of the Division for Early Childhood, 9,* 38–48.

Article examines the evolution of family involvement in early intervention over the last decade in an attempt to understand its current status. The authors note six critical ways in which the implementation of family intervention strategies have been thwarted. Pertinent research is considered; implications for the future are drawn.

Bickman, L., & Weatherford, D. (Eds.). (1986). *Evaluating early intervention programs for severely handicapped children and their families.* Austin, TX: PRO-ED.

Compilation of papers (from a "working conference" on early intervention programs for severely handicapped children held at the John F. Kennedy Center for Research on Education and Human Development) which explores the issue of evaluating program effectiveness relative to impact on family functioning. Experts in the areas of mental retardation, policymaking, and evaluation discuss programs and population, evaluation and design, measurement, and policy and utilization in an effort to suggest methods for determining whether early education for severely handicapped children works. Consideration is given to: what should be evaluated; how and why evaluation should be conducted; how public policy should be informed; and what public, educational, and scientific interests must be taken into account.

Brewer, G.D., & Kakalik, J.S. (1979). *Handicapped children: Strategies for improving services.* New York: McGraw-Hill.

Book based on a 1972 Rand Corporation study that evaluated federal and state programs providing assistance to handicapped children and youth ages 0–21. The three sections include: 1) an overview of the handicapped youth population and aspects of the system which serves it, and a summary of overall findings and recommendations for service improvement; 2) a detailed examination of nine types of service needs; and 3) a summary of results from a survey of families with handicapped children involved in services. In an epilogue, the authors describe their efforts to disseminate study results and to encourage implementation of recommended policy changes.

Carta, J.J., & Greenwood, C.R. (1985). Ecobehavioral assessment: A methodology for expanding the evaluation of early intervention programs. *Topics in Early Childhood Special Education, 5*(2), 88–104.

Article endorses an expanded approach in evaluating early intervention programs. A review of current evaluating methods reveals that past research has been limited to singular outcomes. In light of this determination, an ecobehavioral approach to evaluation, based on behavioral ecology, applied behavioral analysis, and process-product research, is recommended. This type of approach is seen as more holistic and consequently an improvement in the evaluation of efficacy studies.

Casto, G., White, K., & Taylor, C. (1983). An early intervention research institute: Studies of the efficacy and cost effectiveness of early intervention at Utah State. *Journal of the Division for Early Childhood, 7, 5–17.*

Description of the Early Intervention Research Institute (EIRI) which will use meta-analysis techniques to review and integrate existing early intervention research. Discussed are the EIRI's meta-analysis strategies which include developing a model for analyzing cost-effectiveness of early intervention programs. This model will be applied to the study of intervention in home-based and center-based programs. Also described are the EIRI's other activities, including a longitudinal study to determine effects of early intervention with young hearing impaired children.

✓Fewell, R.R., & Vadasy, P.F. (1987). Measurement issues in studies of efficacy. *Topics in Early Childhood Special Education, 7(2), 85–96.*

Examination of the ways in which the goals of early intervention have grown and of the ways in which the effectiveness of these efforts is measured. A historical overview of measurement approaches is presented and critiqued. Problems of relying only on child outcomes are noted; more appropriate measurement approaches are discussed.

Garland, C., Stone, N.W., Swanson, J., & Woodruff, G. (Eds.). (1981). *Early intervention for children with special needs and their families: Findings and recommendations.* Monmouth, OR: Western States Technical Assistance Resource

(WESTAR). (ERIC Document Reproduction Service No. 207 278)

Documentation designed to review the need for early intervention and recommend directions for establishing service delivery systems for children with special needs (ages birth to three) and their families. Issues regarding early intervention programs are discussed, including effectiveness and impact on development, family involvement, and cost effectiveness. Also included is a proposal outlining a national comprehensive service delivery program and its implications for local, state and federal action.

Guralnick, M.J., & Bennett, F.C. (Eds.). (1987). *The effectiveness of early intervention for at-risk and handicapped children*. San Diego: Academic Press.

Review of the existing literature evaluating the effectiveness of early intervention efforts organized by disability and at-risk category: environmentally at risk; increased biologic risk; cognitive and general developmental delays; motor handicaps, language and communication disorders; autism; visual impairments; and hearing impaired. Research in each area is discussed, and tabular summaries of information are included in each section. A final chapter looks toward areas for future research and examines six issues likely to have an impact on early intervention: the role of parents; the expectation of outcomes; practice models; motivational, social, and emotional factors; training; continuity and long-term effects; and biomedical issues and non-standard interventions.

Lazar, I., & Darlington, R.B. (1982). Lasting effects of early education: A report from the Consortium for Longitudinal Studies. *Monographs of the Society for Research in Child Development, 47* (2–3, Serial No. 195).

Report from a study assessing effects of early education on children from low-income families. In 1976, twelve investigators who carried out independent programs in the 1960's (members of the Consortium for Longitudinal Studies) collaborated in an analysis of common data from their original studies and a follow-up of their subjects. Outcome measures were related to children's school competence, performance on intelligence and achievement tests, attitudes and values, as well as to the impact of early childhood programs on families. Long-term effectiveness is considered, as are program effects among subgroups of the low-income population. The authors discuss the study's educational, social and economic significance, and implications of the study for social policy.

Meisels, S.J. (1985). The efficacy of early intervention: Why are we still asking this question? *Topics in Early Childhood Special Education, 5*(2), 1–11.

Article notes that conclusions are often drawn regarding efficacy without consideration of the basic assumptions underlying early intervention programs. Four major assumptions are clarified in order to consider the global questions of efficacy. Determination is that the efficacy question is still being asked for two reasons: that not enough attention is paid to the critical issues of theory, strategies, measurement, and selection criteria; and that the child must be considered in relation to the family.

Mott, S.E., Fewell, R.R., Lewis, M., Meisels, S.J., Shonkoff, J.P., & Simeonsson, R.J. (1986). Methods for assessing child and family outcomes in early childhood special education programs: Some views from the field. *Topics in Early Childhood Special Education, 6*(2), 1–15.

Summary of a 1985 conference that examined the needs of early intervention programs as well as those of the research community with regard to developing instruments for assessing outcomes. Emphasis is on special education programs for children from birth to five years of age. Recommendations are given for methods of determining measurement selection, child outcome measures, and family outcome measures. These recommendations are made by five leading professionals in the field of early childhood special education: Simeonsson, Fewell, Lewis, Meisels, and

Shonkoff. Advantages and disadvantages of measures are discussed.

Provence, S., & Naylor, A. (1983). See annotation in category C.

Sheehan, R. (1981). Issues in documenting early intervention with infants and parents. *Topics in Early Childhood Special Education, 1*(3), 67–75.

Discussion of issues to be considered prior to any data collection or analysis in documenting the effects of early intervention. These issues include the relationship between goals, measures and psychometric concerns; the timing of data collection or analysis; and the linearity of relationships between parent and infant data. Sample data from one typical intervention program (the Early Start Program) are examined throughout the article.

Sheehan, R., & Keogh, B.K. (1982). Design and analysis in the evaluation of early childhood special education programs. *Topics in Early Childhood Special Education, 1* (4), 81–88.

Overview of approaches to evaluation of early childhood special education programs. The rationale for program evaluation is discussed, as are evaluation models and some problems that evaluation poses for early childhood special educators. These include problems related to research designs and analyses. The authors identify three "state-of-the-art" research designs and describe their appropriateness and limitations. The need for a reconsideration of approaches to evaluation is explained, and directions, changes and alternative approaches are recommended.

Simeonsson, R.J., Cooper, D.H., & Scheiner, A.P. (1982). A review and analysis of the effectiveness of early intervention programs. *Pediatrics, 69,* 635–641.

Review of twenty-seven research studies that describe early intervention for biologically impaired infants and young children. The studies were analyzed regarding characteristics of the populations involved, the nature of settings, treatment and evaluation components, and any evidence supporting the effectiveness of early intervention. An analysis was made of the extent to which the studies met scientific criteria for research, citing differences in the effectiveness of intervention between statistical evidence and clinical observations. Implications of the differences noted in the analysis are discussed.

Tjossem, T.D. (Ed.). (1976). *Intervention strategies for high risk infants and young children.* Baltimore: University Park Press.

Compilation of presentations (from a 1974 conference cosponsored by the President's Committee on Mental Retardation and the Association for Childhood Education International) providing a comprehensive perspective of new concepts and developments regarding early intervention. Utilizing an interdisciplinary panel of authorities, the volume includes reports on: research efforts affecting early intervention programs; the early identification of high risk infants; selected demonstration projects; the state of the art in service delivery, pediatric training, and nursing in relation to at-risk infants and early education; and two international early intervention efforts.

White, K.R. (1986). Efficacy of early intervention. *Journal of Special Education, 19,* 401–416.

Paper addresses the dilemma of the efficacy of early intervention: what to do given that government is mandating more services in a time of diminishing resources. Using the six steps of scientific inquiry, an attempt is made to ascertain what is known and what might be done. After an analysis of over 300 studies, it is concluded that early intervention appears to have positive effects, but that good and consistent research, particularly regarding the long-term impact of specific types of intervention, is wanting. The field must be motivated to ensure that research will have a positive impact on policy decisions concerning early intervention services.

Zigler, E.F., & Balla, D. (1982). Selecting outcome variables in evaluations of early childhood special education programs.

*Topics in Early Childhood Special Education, 1*(4), 11–22. Description of outcome variables to be included in evaluating preschool programs for children with handicaps. Issues are examined that need to be considered in selecting variables, including level of children's impairments; specific changes intended by programs; intensity and duration of programs; longitudinal study difficulties; and unintended program effects. The authors discuss program evaluation variables in terms of the child (IQ, academic achievement, social competence, motivation, personality, and physical health and well-being), the family, and society.

## G. PARENT AUTHORS

Butler, A.B. (1983). There's something wrong with Michael: A pediatrician-mother's perspective. *Pediatrics, 71*, 446–448.

Personal account, by a pediatrician, describing her emotions and experiences as a mother of a developmentally disabled child. The author recounts her feelings of denial, anger, and guilt, and describes how they affected her attitude toward many things, including her child's development, medical procedures and testing, health care providers, friends and colleagues, events during the pregnancy, her family, and her patients and their families. Also included are her insights regarding physicians' treatment of handicapped children and their families.

*Equals in this partnership: Parents of disabled and at-risk infants and toddlers speak to professionals.* (1985). Washington, DC: National Center for Clinical Infant Programs.

A booklet developed from conference talks by a variety of parents about their experiences with special needs children, as well as by two professionals who have focused on issues of parent-professional relationships. While the parents describe their own experiences with their children, the focus is on service issues and the special nature of parent-professional interactions. The parents include: Julianne Beckett, Page Gould, Fern Kupfer, Lenette Moses, and Ann Oster.

The professionals include Kathryn Barnard and Lisbeth Vincent.

Featherstone, H. (1981). *A difference in the family: Life with a disabled child.* New York: Penguin Books.

Description of the common features of families having a child with a disability, based on a synthesis of varied experiences. The author, a member of one such family, draws from her own experiences, parent group discussions, and other first-person accounts to look closely at some common themes—fear, anger, guilt, and marital stress—that can be part of such family experiences. Although describing many special characteristics, the author emphasizes the basic normality of the families, and the insights, triumphs, and acceptance possible for family members.

Harrison, H., & Kositsky, A. (1983). *The premature baby book: A parents' guide to coping and caring in the first years.* New York: St. Martin's Press.

Catalogue of information, guidance and support for the parents of premature infants. Fully illustrated, the volume covers topics ranging from the history of premature infant care and detailed information about medical conditions and therapies, to instructions for knitting preemie clothes. Included also are lists of support groups, glossaries of trade names and technical terms, and a discussion of long-term prognoses. Of special interest are the first-person stories and pictures throughout the volume. The book is relevant for professionals as well as parents.

Kupfer, F. (1988). *Before and after Zachariah.* Chicago: Academy Chicago.

Story of one family's experience with a severely disabled child. Written by Zachariah's mother, this is an intimate story, told bravely, honestly and vividly, of the prolonged period of unnamed fear, the confirmation of those fears, and the chronic complex strains that threatened this family.

Pizzo, P. (1983). See annotation in category C.

Stinson, R., & Stinson, P. (1983). *The long dying of baby Andrew*. Boston: Little, Brown.

The history, in the form of a husband-wife joint diary, of the birth and crisis-filled 6 months of life for the authors' premature son. While a deeply personal and often angry story, it also gives a detailed account of the medical complexities, the conflicts between professionals, between professionals and parents, and of the moral conflicts over the child's management. With painful realism, it also makes clear the way an extended crisis challenges the structure of a family.

Turnbull, A.P., & Turnbull, H.R. (Eds.). (1985). *Parents speak out: Then and now* (2nd ed.). Columbus, OH: Charles E. Merrill.

A new edition to this classic book of essays by parents, many of whom are also professionals in the area of services for people with disabilities. This has an especially interesting approach to revision. The work is divided into three sections. The first contains essays from the original book, followed by "updated" additions, with comments on changes since the previous edition, new insights on services, philosophy, and goals. A second section contains two of the original parent essays without updates, and a third section contains three new essays by parents, including one by Senator Lowell Weicker. In additions to the updates, photographs and questions to guide exploration of some of the issues discussed are provided for each contribution.

## H. POLICY

Bricker, D. (1987). Impact of research on social policy for handicapped infants and children. *Journal of the Division for Early Childhood, 11,* 98–105.

Paper examines research on social policy as it affects handicapped infants and children. A definition of social policy is given; steps in the development of social policy and the factors influencing it are outlined. The reciprocal nature of research and social policy, and the impact of research application are also discussed. Recommendations are given for using research to forge social policy to benefit handicapped children.

Clarke-Stewart, A. (1977). *Child care in the family: A review of research and some propositions for policy.* San Diego: Academic Press.

A Carnegie Council on Children publication reviewing research on relations between child development and parental care and offering a number of propositions for child-care policy. The author notes that the review is not a comprehensive survey of all social science research on child development; psychological and behavioral research is emphasized (sociological and economic research is not included), and discussion is limited to the immediate effects of families on children's behavior. Also included is an examination of the difficulties and dangers of using current research for formulating propositions for policy.

deLone, R.H. (1982). Early childhood development as a policy goal: An overview of choices. In L. Bond & J. Joffe (Eds.), *Facilitating infant and early childhood development* (pp. 485–502). Hanover, NH: University of New England Press.

Overview of theoretical perspectives involved in designing public policy to facilitate early childhood development. The relationship between socioeconomic factors and development is discussed, and the author proposes the need for a developmental theory that takes into account socioeconomic factors as a basis for policy. Two policy options that accommodate the socioeconomic and development relationship are described, and their implications and appropriateness as bases for public policy are explored.

*Evaluating service programs for infants, toddlers and their families: A guide for policy makers and funders.* (1987). Washington, DC: National Center for Clinical Infant Programs.

Booklet provides evaluation guidelines for persons involved in developing policy, allocating funds, and providing services to enhance the healthy development of children from birth to 3 years of age and their families. Steps for program, process, and outcome evaluations are given; suggestions for using the information obtained are given.

Garwood, S.G. (Ed.). (1984). Social policy and young handicapped children. *Topics in Early Childhood Special Education, 4* (1).

Issue examining topics and concerns regarding social policy and its effect on the care and education of handicapped children. Included are articles about: what social policy is; pertinent past and present legislation; trends, the state of the art, and issues in early childhood special education; the federal role in serving special needs children; a policy analysis of PL 94-142; the need for policy protecting abused or seriously ill infants and children; effects of government and agency involvement on family authority; difficulties in gathering data needed for decision making; and interaction among special education advocacy groups.

Gliedman, J., & Roth, W. (1980). *The unexpected minority.* New York: Harcourt Brace Jovanovich.

A Carnegie Council on Children publication analyzing aspects of childhood disability from the perspective that persons with handicaps are an oppressed minority group. Similarities between America's past oppression of certain social groups and the current treatment of persons with handicaps are discussed, as are psychologists' methods for studying handicapped children's development, the education and health professional's role in providing services to handicapped children and their parents, and the employment problem of present and future generations of disabled adults. Included among the appendices are essays regarding the medical needs of handicapped children as well as the role of preventive medicine with regard to disabilities, and the need for a national health insurance plan for defraying medical and nonmedical costs of raising a handicapped child.

Haskins, R., & Adams, D. (Eds.). (1983). *Parent education and public policy.* Norwood, NJ: Ablex.

Third volume in the Child and Family series examining research on the effects of parent education, its implications, and policy recommendations. Subject areas include: parent education and public policy background; research on selected aspects of parent education and participation in programs involving handicapped and nonhandicapped children; issues associated with parent programs; and a synthesis of findings, accompanied by policy recommendations.

Hobbs, N., Dokecki, P.R., Hoover-Dempsey, K.V., Moroney, R.M., Shayne, M.W., & Weeks, K.H. (1984). *Strengthening families: Strategies for improved child care and parent education.* San Francisco: Jossey-Bass.

Book presenting a 5-year project that addressed contemporary needs of families. Public policy options with regard to child care and parent education are proposed, and strategies to promote the well-being of individuals, families, and communities are recommended. The authors recommend and discuss the implementation of child care and parent education services through the public education system.

*Infants can't wait.* (1986). Washington, DC: National Center for Clinical Infant Programs.

Review of the developmental needs of children in the first 3 years of life, support available in the U.S., and needs that are not being met. Suggests two initiatives for improvement: establishment of a basic floor of integrated services for all infants and toddlers and their families; and expansion of comprehensive, integrated services for infants and toddlers with special health and developmental problems or disabling conditions and for their families. A companion booklet, *Infants can't wait: The numbers,* lends statistical support to the positions held in this pamphlet.

Schorr, L.B., Miller, C.A., & Fine, A. (1986). The social-policy context for families today. In M.W. Yogman & T.B. Brazelton (Eds.), *In support of families* (pp. 242–255). Cambridge, MA: Harvard University Press.

Essay discusses the issue of caring for young children in light of the complexity of recent social changes that have taken place in this country. Aspects considered include: health status and well-being; supports to improve outcomes; and preschool interventions. Recommendations are given for community, state, and national programs.

Smith, B.J. (1980). *Policy options related to the provision of appropriate early intervention services for very young exceptional children and their families.* Reston, VA: The Council for Exceptional Children. (ERIC Document Reproduction Service No. 224 264)

Report (from the Policy Options Project of The Council for Exceptional Children) analyzing policy issues concerning the delivery of services to young handicapped children and their families. The value of, and need for, early intervention are discussed, as are current policies related to it. Topics in preschool services are examined and include: the population to be served, the scope of services, the service providers, resource availability, and the effects of mandatory service provision compared with the effects of incentive, or permissive, provision. Also included are policy options relative to each topic.

Weissbourd, B., & Musick, J.S. (Eds.). (1981). See annotation in category I.

Zigler, E.F., & Finn, M. (1982). A vision of child care in the 1980s. In L. Bond & E. Joffe (Eds.), *Facilitating infant and early childhood development* (pp. 443–465). Hanover, NH: University of New England Press.

Zigler, E.F., Kagan, S.L., & Klugman, E. (Eds.). (1983). *Children, families, and government: Perspectives on American social policy.* New York: Cambridge University Press.

Volume examining the development of social policies for children and families. Topics include: the history of federal policy for children and families; differing perspectives on policy development; the policy-making process at federal and state levels; influences on the policy-making process;

the translation of social problems into social policies; and future issues for child and family policies. Contributors include authorities in child development, education, political science, psychiatry, psychology and social policy.

## I. OTHER

Bennett, F.C. (1982). The pediatrician and the interdisciplinary process. *Exceptional Children, 48,* 306–314.

Essay examining issues related to the pediatrician's role in the interdisciplinary process. The author describes the functions and responsibilities for the pediatrician as they relate to various interdisciplinary settings, including the child diagnostic clinic, the neonatal intensive care unit and follow-up clinic, specialty clinics serving handicapped children, and the school. The impact of the interdisciplinary process on physician training and clinical research is discussed, as are problems associated with interdisciplinary function. Also included are the author's suggestions for overcoming the problems.

*Children Today.* See The Earliest Years [Special issue], 1981.

Division of Maternal and Child Health, Department of Health and Human Services. (1980). *Guidelines for early intervention programs* (based on a conference, Health Issues in Early Intervention Programs, Washington, DC). Salt Lake City: College of Nursing, University of Utah.

Document (from a 1980 conference sponsored by the Division of Maternal and Child Health, the College of Nursing of the University of Utah, and the School of Public Health of the University of Hawaii) intended for practitioners in programs for infants from birth to 3 with discernible handicaps and for their families. Included are: three papers on intervention regarding the state of the art in infancy intervention, child change in programs, and parent involvement; a review of contemporary theory regarding intervention-related topics; and recommended guidelines for intervention programs. The appendices contain profiles of two intervention programs, a list of staffing considerations, and a list of conference participants.

The Earliest Years [Special issue]. (1981). *Children Today, 10* (4).

Issue focusing on early promotion of physical and mental health in children. Included are articles concerning behavioral assessment of newborns; demonstration of infant behavior; primary prevention in infancy; effects of environmental toxins on the developing infant; a hospital family care center for sick infants and their families; adaptive and psychopathologic patterns in infancy and early childhood; preventive intervention in multi-risk factor families; the social-cultural context of malnutrition; obstacles to early infant assessment and treatment; and the humanizing of neonatal intensive care units.

Farel, A.M., Bailey, D.B., Jr., & O'Donnell, K.J. (1987). A new approach for training infant intervention specialists. *Infant Mental Health Journal, 8,* 76–85.

Outline of a new approach for training infant interventionists that advocates interdisciplinary education in maternal and child health and special education. Improvement of infant specialists' skills is emphasized, particularly in the areas of assessing, planning, and intervening on behalf of infants at risk, the ability to work with families, and the ability to make use of community resources. The need for shared responsibility and integrated awareness among professionals and agencies that identify and serve vulnerable children is also discussed, as is the changing social and political climate within which these needs are being addressed.

Field, T.M. (Ed.). (1980). *High-risk infants and children: Adult and peer interactions.* San Diego: Academic Press.

Collection of studies describing social interactions of infants and children at risk due to handicapping conditions or unfavorable caregiving environments. Included are studies concerning early interactions of these infants and children with their parents, as well as studies examining interactions of at-risk children with their teachers and peers. At-risk infants and children included those diagnosed as having psychiatric problems, failures to thrive, and perceptual-motor handicaps, as well as those experiencing abuse, family disruptions, premature birth, or perinatal complications.

Garwood, S.G. (Ed.). (1986). Chronically ill children. *Topics in Early Childhood Special Education, 5*(4).

Issue focuses on the specialized needs of "other health impaired" (OHI) or chronically ill children. Articles included are: "Chronically ill children: An overview," "Chronically ill children in early childhood education programs"; "Developmental issues in chronic illness: Implications and applications"; "Parents' perspectives on the school experiences of children with cancer"; "Issues in research on the young chronically ill child"; "Issues in the financing of care for chronically ill children and their families"; "Promoting communication between health care providers and educators of chronically ill children"; "Institutional and professional attitudes: Dilemmas for the chronically ill child"; and "Resources available to teachers working with chronically ill children."

Garwood, S.G., & Fewell, R.R. (Eds.). (1982). *Educating handicapped infants: Issues in development and intervention.* Rockville, MD: Aspen Publishers.

Volume concerning infant education, intended for educators with beginning involvement in infant education. Discussions are concerned mainly with issues in infant development, including theories, concepts and methodologies, physical growth, perception and cognition, and social development. The roles of differing disciplines in facilitating development of handicapped infants are examined, involving such areas as assessment, the team approach to infant education, health care, developmental therapy, service models, curricula, family adaptation, and the evaluation of intervention programs.

*Guidelines for early intervention programs.* See Division of Maternal and Child Health, Department of Health and Human Services, 1980.

Guralnick, M.J., Bennett, F.C., Heiser, K.E., & Richardson, H.B., Jr. (1987). Training future primary care pediatricians to serve handicapped children and their families. *Topics in Early Childhood Special Education,* 6(4), 1–11.

Outline of a curriculum designed to prepare primary care pediatricians for the crucial role they play in screening and identifying developmental problems. Since evaluations have indicated that these professionals are perhaps ill-prepared to make quality developmental assessments, inclusion of a clinical rotation in developmental pediatrics during their residency is recommended. Description of such a curriculum is presented with the results of both subjective and objective evaluations of such a training program.

Healy, A. (1983). *The needs of children with disabilities: A comprehensive view.* Iowa City: Division of Developmental Disabilities, The University of Iowa.

Monograph (from a series of five) examining the role of health care services for children with disabilities in the context of the child's total service needs. Sections present an overview of the history of health care for children with disabilities, an examination of topics regarding health service needs (including disabled population characteristics; service areas; the role of primary, secondary, and tertiary health care services; community support services; linkage between services; and training and research needs), and a discussion of service coordination.

Healy, A., & Lewis-Beck, J.A. (1987). *The Iowa health care guidelines project* (series). Iowa City: The University of Iowa.

Four separate publications with guidelines for four separate groups involved with the care of chronically ill or disabled children. The project goal was to promote active family involvement, improved communication between professionals and families, written service plans for children and families, access to health care information for families, and family-centered care. There is a booklet of guidelines for families, one for physicians, one for social workers, and one for therapists. The family guidelines were written by a panel of representative parents. The professional guidelines were each developed by panels of professionals from the respective disciplines. Each includes both general guidelines and specific action steps.

McDonald, A.C., Carson, K.L., Palmer, D.J., & Slay, T. (1982). See annotation in category C.

Miller, C.A. (1984). The health of children: A crisis of ethics. *Pediatrics, 73, 550–558.*

Essay concerning the health status of children in this country. The availability (under current programs and policies) of essential health care services and benefits to all children is examined, as are problems that stand in the way of improving health care services. The author discusses issues related to the role of federal, state and local governments in providing and allocating these services. Also described is the role of public service programs in ensuring that the needs of children are addressed in a way that will not weaken private medical practice.

Olds, D.L. (1982). The Prenatal/Early Infancy Project: An ecological approach to prevention of developmental disabilities. In J. Belsky (Ed.), *In the beginning: Readings on infancy* (pp. 270–285). New York: Columbia University Press.

Description of the Prenatal/Early Infancy Project, a prevention program designed to aid families at risk for having children with health or developmental problems. The nature of the program, which emphasizes the relationship between the family environment, parental behavior, and infant health, is explained, as are its activities, which include nurse home visitations during and after pregnancy, and the development of community support systems for the family. The focus of the program is educating parents, involving relatives and friends, and linking parents with formal services. Also considered is the importance of ecological theory in analyzing the program's effectiveness.

Phillips, D.C. (1980). What do the researcher and the practitioner have to offer each other? *Educational Researcher, 9* (12), 17–20.

Examination of the use of social science research by practitioners. The author cites evidence that a gap exists between research and practice. The need for linkage between the two is illustrated, as are complications involved in making "linking premises" and assumptions. Also considered are successful practitioners' contributions to research.

Ramey, C.T., Trohanis, P.L., & Hostler, S.L. (1982). An introduction. In C.T. Ramey & P.L. Trohanis (Eds.), *Finding and educating high-risk and handicapped infants* (pp. 1–17). Austin, TX: PRO-ED.

Introductory chapter providing background information regarding infant development and services. Topics briefly covered include: a transactional model of development and its implications for infant education; purposes of remediation and prevention programs; the history of children's rights as reflected by changes in legal, educational and health care practices; concepts of risk and of handicaps. Signs of progress in the areas of policy making, medical technology and practice, research, demonstration programs, training efforts, and advocacy are also presented.

Shonkoff, J.P. (1983). A perspective on pediatric training. In J.A. Mulick & S.M. Pueschel (Eds.), *Parent-professional partnerships in developmental disability services* (pp. 75–88). Cambridge, MA: Academic Guild.

Essay examining pediatric training with regard to the needs of developmentally disabled children and their families. The author explores the history of traditional physician education, notes changes needed to foster effective parent-professional partnerships, and suggests ways to improve pediatric training.

Shonkoff, J.P., Dworkin, P.H., Leviton, A., & Levine, M.D. (1979). Primary care approaches to developmental disabilities. *Pediatrics, 64,* 506–514.

Report of a study designed to describe current attitudes and approaches to developmental disabilities in primary pediatric health care settings. Ninety-seven pediatricians working in health services were interviewed. The authors conclude that pediatricians need more rigorous training in the developmental aspects of child health, and more precise methods for doing developmental assessments and for measuring the effects of various interventions.

Stack, J.M. (Ed.). (1982). *The special infant: An interdisciplinary approach to the optimal development of infants.* New York: Human Sciences Press.

Presentations (from a 1979 conference of the Michigan Association for Infant Mental Health) examining topics related to development and assessment, families of special infants, and attachment and separation. Several chapters focus on characteristics and problems of children with physical or emotional handicaps; others examine the effect of a child's handicap on the family and ways to assist families. The nature of a few specific problems in attachment and separation is illustrated through clinical examples.

Thornton, S.M., & Frankenburg, W.K. (Eds.). (1983). *Child health care communications: Enhancing interactions among professionals, parents and children.* Johnson & Johnson Baby Products Company Pediatric Round Table Series (No. 8). Somerville, NJ: Johnson & Johnson Baby Products Company.

Collection of papers examining communication in child health services. Subject areas include: Issues to be addressed if health care communication is to improve, focusing on the needs and capabilities of children and their families, and the systems that serve them; strategies for teaching parents, children, and professionals to communicate more effectively; and recommendations for public policy and for the education of health care professionals which promote better communication. The appendices include guidelines for improving health care communications.

Walker, J.A. (1982). Social interactions of handicapped infants. In D.D. Bricker (Ed.), *Intervention with at-risk and handicapped infants: From research to application* (pp. 217–232). Austin, TX: PRO-ED.

Chapter focusing on the potential use of theory and research models derived from work with nonhandicapped infants for describing social interactions between handicapped infants and their caregivers. Specific patterns of such interactions are examined, as are some more general characteristics of social interactions in infancy. Also included are questions, problems, and proposed solutions to consider when applying theory and research models.

Weiser, M.G. (1982). *Group care and education of infants and toddlers.* Columbus, OH: Charles E. Merrill.

Textbook for prospective teachers and caregivers involved with children from birth to thirty-six months. Topics include: principles of early development and related goals and objectives for care and early education; safety, nutrition, and health components of infant-toddler care; learning and teaching in the developmental-educational curriculum; and application of theories of child development, care, and education to practices and to development of physical and social environments for group care. Quality group care characteristics are further illustrated through descriptions of typical days for three children.

Weissbourd, B., & Musick, J.S. (Eds.). (1981). *Infants: Their social environments.* Washington, DC: National Association for the Education of Young Children.

Book examining issues regarding social and caregiving environments for infants and young children. Among the topics covered are recent infancy research, assessment of infants' developmental needs, group day care, a curriculum for infants and toddlers, a program for infants with developmental delays, the Parent Behavior Progression assessment instrument, an intervention program aimed at high-risk families, the changing roles and attitudes of mothers and fathers, social support for parents, and social policy issues affecting infants. Included among the contributors are Bromwich, Dittman, Honig, Ramey, Sawin, and the editors.

Werner, E.E., & Smith, R.S. (1982). *Vulnerable but invincible: A longitudinal study of resilient children and youth*. New York: McGraw-Hill.

Report from a 20-year study of the children of Kauai, focusing on their biological, social, and psychological vulnerabilities and their capacities to cope effectively. The authors present an overview of childhood vulnerability, and sex differences in vulnerability and resilience are examined. Characteristics within the child and the caregiving environment were identified that differentiated high-risk but resilient children from those who developed serious learning and behavioral problems. Also considered are the interrelationships between child and caregiver variables contributing to resiliency in high-risk children, with selected case studies included throughout the book.

Wolfensberger, W. (1983). Social role valorization: A proposed new term for the principle of normalization. *Mental Retardation, 21,* 234–239.

Essay suggesting the term "social role valorization" as a replacement for "the principle of normalization." The history of, and problems with, the term "normalization" are discussed, as is a new conceptualization of normalization and its role in influencing the proposed name change. The concept of "social role valorization" is analyzed.

# University of Iowa Birth-to-Three Project
## Categorized Bibliography

Categories:
- A.  Child Development and Research
- B.  Social Support
- C.  Parent/Family Focus (needs, involvement, education)
- D.  Neonatal Issues, Intervention, Follow-Up
- E.  Identification, Assessment, Intervention
- F.  Early Intervention Efficacy (outcomes, reviews, commentaries)
- G.  Parent Authors
- H.  Policy
- I.  Other

### A.  CHILD DEVELOPMENT AND RESEARCH

Anastasiow, N.J. (Ed.). (1981). *New directions for exceptional children: No. 5. Socioemotional development*. San Francisco: Jossey-Bass.

Anastasiow, N.J. (1986). *Development and disability: A psychobiological analysis for special educators*. Baltimore: Paul H. Brookes Publishing Co.

Baum, A., & Singer, J.E. (Eds.). (1982). *Handbook of psychology and health* (Vol. 2). Hillsdale, NJ: Lawrence Erlbaum Associates.

Beckwith, L. (1980). The influence of caregiver-infant interaction on development. In E. Sell (Ed.), *Follow-up of the high-risk newborn: A practical approach* (pp. 75–91). Springfield, IL: Charles C Thomas.

Bond, L., & Joffe, J. (Eds.). (1982). *Facilitating infant and early childhood development.* Hanover, NH: University of New England Press.

Bower, G.H. (Ed.). (1980). *The psychology of learning and motivation* (Vol. 14). San Diego: Academic Press.

Brazelton, T.B., & Yogman, M. (Eds.). (1986). *Affective development in infancy.* Norwood, NJ: Ablex.

Casey, P.H., & Bradley, R.H. (1982). The impact of the home environment on children's development: Clinical relevance for the pediatrician. *Journal of Developmental and Behavioral Pediatrics, 3,* 146–152.

Cath, S.H., Gurwitt, A.R., & Ross, J.H. (Eds.). (1982). *Father and child: Developmental and clinical perspectives.* Boston: Little, Brown.

Chess, S., & Thomas, A. (1985). Temperamental differences: A critical concept in child health care. *Pediatric Nursing, 11,* 167–172.

Emde, R.N., Gaensbauer, T.J., & Harmon, R.J. (1976). Emotional expression in infancy: A biobehavioral study. *Psychological Issues, 10*(1), Monograph 37. Madison, CT: International Universities Press.

Emde, R.N., & Harmon, R.J. (1982). *The development of attachment and affiliative systems.* New York: Plenum.

Emde, R.N., & Harmon, R.J. (1984). *Continuities and discontinuities in development.* New York: Plenum.

Farran, D.C., & McKinney, J.D. (Eds.). (1986). *Risk in intellectual and psychosocial development.* San Diego: Academic Press.

Gallagher, J.J., & Ramey, C.T. (1987). *The malleability of children.* Baltimore: Paul H. Brookes Publishing Co.

Greenspan, S.I., & Greenspan, N.T. (1985). *First feelings:*

*Milestones in the emotional development of your baby and child.* New York: Viking.

Kagan, J. (1981). *The second year: The emergence of self-aware-ness.* Cambridge: Harvard University Press.

Kagan, J., & Greenspan, S.I. (1986). Milestones of development: A dialogue. *Zero to Three, VI(5),* 1–9.

Lewis, M., & Rosenblum, L.A. (Eds.). (1981). *The uncommon child.* New York: Plenum.

Minde, K. (1986). Bonding and attachment: Its relevance for the present-day clinician. *Developmental Medicine and Child Neurology, 28,* 803–806.

Mitchell, K., & Mills, N.M. (1983). See full citation in category D.

Mussen, P.H. (Ed.). (1983). *Handbook of child psychology* (4th ed.). New York: John Wiley & Sons.

Mussen, P.H. (Ed.). (1983). *Handbook of child psychology* (4th ed.): *Vol. 4. Socialization, personality and social development.* New York: John Wiley & Sons.

Plunkett, J.W., Meisels, S.J., Stiefel, G.S., Pasick, P.L., & Roloff, D.W. (1986). Patterns of attachment among preterm infants of varying biological risk. *Journal of the American Academy of Child Psychiatry, 25,* 794–800.

Schiefelbusch, R.L., & Lloyd, L.L. (Eds.). (1974). *Language perspectives: Acquisition, retardation, and intervention.* Austin, TX: PRO-ED.

Spieker, S.J. (1986). Patterns of very insecure attachment found in samples of high-risk infants and toddlers. *Topics in Early Childhood Special Education, 6(3),* 37–53.

Stern, D.L. (1985). *The interpersonal world of the infant: A view from psychoanalysis and developmental psychology.* New York: Basic Books.

Stone, N.W., & Chesney, B.H. (1978). Attachment behavior in handicapped infants. *Mental Retardation, 16(1),* 8–12.

Walk, R.D. (1981). *Perceptual development.* Monterey, CA: Brooks/Cole Publishing.

Washington, J., Klaus, M., & Goldberg, S. (1986). Temperament in preterm infants: Style and stability. *Journal of the American Academy of Child Psychiatry, 25,* 493–502.

Wasserman, G.A., Lennon, M.C., Allen, R., & Shilansky, M. (1987). Contributors to attachment in normal and physically handicapped infants. *Journal of the American Academy of Child and Adolescent Psychiatry, 26,* 9–15.

## B. SOCIAL SUPPORT

Bee, H.L., Hammond, M.A., Eyres, S.J., Barnard, K.E., & Snyder, C. (1986). The impact of parental life change on the early development of children. *Research in Nursing & Health, 9,* 65–74.

Cena, S., & Caro, F.G. (1984). See full citation in category H.

Dunst, C.J., Jenkins, V., & Trivette, C.M. (1984). The family support scale: Reliability and validity. *Journal of Individual, Family, and Community Wellness, 1*(4), 45–52.

Dunst, C.J., Leet, H.E., & Trivette, C.M. (1988). Family resources, personal well-being, and early intervention. *Journal of Special Education, 22*(1), 108–116.

Dunst, C.J., Trivette, C.M., & Cross, A. (1986). Mediating influences of social support: Personal, family and child outcomes. *American Journal of Mental Deficiency, 90,* 403–417.

Dunst, C., Trivette, C., & Deal, A. (1988). *Enabling and empowering families: Principles and guidelines for practice.* Cambridge, MA: Brookline Books.

Mott, S.E., & Casto, G. (1986). *Annotated bibliography of self-report measures of family functioning.* Logan: Utah State University, Early Intervention Research Institute Press. (ERIC Document Reproduction Service No. ED 278 205)

Seitz, V., Rosenbaum, L.K., & Apfel, N.H. (1985). Effects of family support intervention: A 10-year followup. *Child Development, 56,* 376–391.

Tingey, C., Boyd, R., & Casto, G. (1987). See full citation in category C.

Weiss, H., & Jacobs, F. (Eds.). (1988). *Evaluating family programs*. Hawthorne, NY: Aldine.

White, K.R. (1988). Cost analyses in family support programs. In H. Weiss & F. Jacobs (Eds.), *Evaluating family programs* (pp. 429–443). Hawthorne, NY: Aldine.

## C. PARENT/FAMILY FOCUS
(needs, involvement, education)

Bailey, D.B. (1987). Collaborative goal-setting with families: Resolving differences in values and priorities for services. *Topics in Early Childhood Special Education, 7*(2), 59–71.

Bailey, D.B., & Simeonsson, R.J. (1988). Assessing needs of families with handicapped infants: The family needs survey. *Journal of Special Education, 22*(1), 117–127.

Bailey, D.B., Simeonsson, R.J., Isbell, P., Huntington, G.S., Winton, P.J., Comfort, M., & Helm, J. (1988). Inservice training in family assessment and goal-setting for early intervention: Outcomes and issues. *Journal of the Division for Early Childhood, 12*, 126–136.

Bailey, D.B., Simeonsson, R.J., Winton, P.J., Huntington, G.S., Comfort, M., Isbell, P., O'Donnell, K.J., & Helm, J.M. (1986). Family-focused intervention: A functional model for planning, implementing, and evaluating individualized family services in early intervention. *Journal of the Division for Early Childhood, 10*, 156–171.

Blacher, J. (Ed.). (1984). *Severely handicapped young children and their families: Research in review*. San Diego: Academic Press.

Bricker, D.D., & Casuso, V. (1979). Family involvement: A critical component of early intervention. *Exceptional Children, 46*, 108–116.

Casto, G. (1986). Family assessment. *DEC Communicator, 12*(3), 1–2.

Casto, G., & Lewis, A. (1984). Parent involvement in infant and preschool programs. *Journal of the Division for Early Childhood, 9,* 49–56.

Causby, V. (1985). The relationship of role sharing and social support to maternal interactions with preschool handicapped children. (Doctoral dissertation, Florida State University, 1985). *Dissertation Abstracts International,* 8513362.

Dunst, C.J., Leet, H.E., & Trivette, C.M. (1988). See full citation in category B.

Dunst, C.J., & Trivette, C.M. (1987). Enabling and empowering families: Conceptual and intervention issues. *School Psychology Review, 16,* 443–456.

Dunst, C., Trivette, C., & Deal A. (1988). See full citation in category B.

Fewell, R.R. (Ed.). (1981). Families of handicapped children. *Topics in Early Childhood Special Education, 1* (3).

Gallagher, J.J. (Ed.). (1980). *New directions for exceptional children: No. 4. Parents and families of handicapped children.* San Francisco: Jossey-Bass.

Hoffman, L.W., Gandelman, R., & Schiffman, H.R. (Eds.). (1982). *Parenting: Its causes and consequences.* Hillsdale, NJ: Lawrence Erlbaum Associates.

Humenick, S.S., & Bugen, L.A. (1981). Correlates of parent-infant interaction: An exploratory study. In R.P. Lederman & B.S. Raff (Eds.), *Perinatal parental behavior* [Birth Defects: Original Article Series, 17(6)] (pp. 181–193). New York: Alan R. Liss.

Macnab, A.J., Sheckter, L.A., Hendry, N.J., Pendray, M.R., & Macnab, G. (1985). Group support for parents of high-risk neonates: An interdisciplinary approach. *Social Work in Health Care, 10*(4), 63–72.

McGonigel, M.J., & Garland, C.W. (1988). The individualized family service plan and the early intervention team: Team and family issues and recommended practices. *Infants and Young Children, 1* (1), 10–21.

McKay, S. (1986). *The assertive approach to childbirth: Using communication and information strategies to increase birthing options.* Minneapolis: International Childbirth Education Association.

Noble, D.N., & Hamilton, A.K. (1981). Families under stress: Perinatal social work. *Health and Social Work, 6,* 28–35.

O'Connor, S.M., Vietze, P.M., Sandler, H.M., Sherrod, K.B., & Altemeier, W.A. (1980). Quality of parenting and the mother-infant relationship following rooming-in. In P.M. Taylor (Ed.), *Parent-infant relationships* (pp. 349–368). Orlando: Grune & Stratton.

Osofsky, H.J., & Osofsky, J.D. (1980). See full citation in category I.

Parke, R.D., Power, T.G., Tinsley, B.R., & Hymel, S. (1980). The father's role in the family system. In P.M. Taylor (Ed.), *Parent-infant relationships* (pp. 117–133). Orlando: Grune & Stratton.

Perry, S.E. (1983). Parents' perceptions of their newborn following structured interactions. *Nursing Research, 32,* 208–212.

Powell, T.H., & Ogle, P.A. (1985). *Brothers & sisters—A special part of exceptional families.* Baltimore: Paul H. Brookes Publishing Co.

Reading, A.E., Cox, D.N., Sledmere, C.M., & Campbell, S. (1984). Psychological changes over the course of pregnancy: A study of attitudes toward the fetus/neonate. *Health Psychology, 3,* 211–221.

Rosenbaum, P.L., Armstrong, R.W., & King, S.M. (1987). Parental attitudes toward children with handicaps: New perspectives with a new measure. *Journal of Developmental and Behavioral Pediatrics, 8,* 327–334.

Russel, F.F. (1985). *Interdisciplinary early intervention for developmentally delayed infants and young children: A fam-*

*ily-oriented approach.* Memphis: Child Development Center, University of Tennessee Center for the Health Sciences.

Sciarillo, W.G., Jr. (1980). Using Hymovich's framework in the family-oriented approach to nursing care. *American Journal of Maternal Child Nursing (MCN)*, 5, 242–248.

Shelton, T.L., Jeppson, E.S., & Johnson, B.H. (1987). *Family-centered care for children with special health care needs* (2nd ed.). (Available from the Association for the Care of Children's Health, 3615 Wisconsin Avenue, N.W., Washington, DC.)

Thomson, M.E., & Kramer, M.S. (1984). Methodologic standards for controlled clinical trials of early contact and maternal-infant behavior. *Pediatrics*, 73, 294–300.

Tingey, C., Boyd, R., & Casto, G. (1987). Parental involvement in early intervention: Becoming a parent plus. *Early Childhood Development and Care*, 28, 91–105.

Trout, M.D. (1983). Birth of a sick or handicapped infant: Impact on the family. *Child Welfare*, 62, 337–348.

World Rehabilitation Fund. See Zucman, E., 1982.

Yang, R.K. (1981). Maternal attitudes during pregnancy and medication during labor and delivery: Methodological considerations. In V.L. Smeriglio (Ed.), *Newborns and parents: Parent-infant contact and newborn sensory stimulation* (pp. 105–116). Hillsdale, NJ: Lawrence Erlbaum Associates.

Zucman, E. (1982). *Childhood disability in the family: Recognizing the added disability* (Monograph No. 14). New York: World Rehabilitation Fund.

## D. NEONATAL ISSUES, INTERVENTION, FOLLOW-UP

Ahmann, E. (1986). *Home care for the high-risk infant.* Rockville, MD: Aspen Publishers.

Als, H., Lawhon, G., Brown, E., Gibes, R., Duffy, F.H., McAnulty, G., & Blickman, J.G. (1986). Individualized behavioral and environmental care for the very low birth weight preterm infant at high risk for bronchopulmonary dysplasia: Neonatal intensive care unit and developmental outcome. *Pediatrics, 78,* 1123–1132.

Amiel-Tison, C., & Grenier, A. (1986). *Neurological assessment during the first year of life.* New York: Oxford University Press.

Bailey, D.B., & Woolery, M. (1984). *Teaching infants and preschoolers with handicaps.* Columbus, OH: Charles E. Merrill.

Barrera, M.E., Cunningham, C.E., & Rosenbaum, P.L. (1986). Low birth weight and home intervention strategies: Preterm infants. *Journal of Developmental and Behavioral Pediatrics, 7,* 361–366.

Beckwith, L., Parmelee, A.H., Cohen, S.E., & Howard, J. (1984). Behavioral and developmental outcome for low birth weight infants [Abstract]. *Journal of Developmental and Behavioral Pediatrics, 5,* 155–156.

Blackburn, S. (1983). Fostering behavioral development of high-risk infants. *JOGN-Nursing, 3* (May-June suppl.), 76s–86s.

Blackman, J. (1986). *Warning signals: Basic criteria for tracking at-risk infants and toddlers.* (Available from the National Center for Clinical Infant Programs, 733 15th Street, N.W., Suite 912, Washington, DC.)

Campbell, S.K. (1983). Effects of developmental intervention in the special care nursery. In D. Routh & M.L. Wolraich (Eds.), *Advances in developmental and behavioral pediatrics* (Vol. 4, pp. 165–179). Greenwich, CT: JAI Press.

Cornell, E.H., & Gottfried, A.W. (1976). Intervention with premature human infants. *Child Development, 47,* 32–39.

Davis, J.A., Richards, M.P.M., & Roberton, N.R.C. (Eds.). (1983). *Parent-baby attachment in premature infants.* New York: St. Martin's Press.

Gaiter, J.L., & Gottfried, A.W. (Eds.). (1985). *Infant stress under intensive care.* Baltimore: University Park Press.

Gibbs, R.M. (1981). Clinical uses of the Brazelton Neonatal Behavioral Assessment Scale in nursing practice. *Pediatric Nursing, 7*(3), 23–26.

Gorski, P.A. (1984). Experiences following premature birth: Stresses and opportunities for infants, parents, and professionals. In J.D. Call, E. Galenson, & R.L. Tyson (Eds.), *Frontiers of infant psychiatry* (Vol. 2, pp. 145–151). New York: Basic Books.

Gorski, P.A. (1984). Handling, heart rate, and health in preterm infants [Abstract]. *Journal of Developmental and Behavioral Pediatrics, 5,* 149.

Gunzenhauser, N. (Ed.) (1987). *Infant stimulation: For whom, what kind, when, and how much?* Johnson & Johnson Baby Products Company Pediatric Round Table Series (No. 13). Somerville, NJ: Johnson & Johnson Baby Products Company.

Harel, S., & Anastasiow, N.J. (Eds.). (1985). *The at-risk infant: Psycho/socio/medical aspects.* Baltimore: Paul H. Brookes Publishing Co.

Honig, A.S. (Ed.). (1986). *Risk factors in infancy.* New York: Gordon & Breach.

Lederman, R.P., Lederman, E., Work, B.A., Jr., & McCann, D.S. (1981). The relationship of maternal prenatal development to progress in labor and fetal newborn health. In R.P. Lederman & B.S. Raff (Eds.), *Perinatal Parental Behavior* [Birth Defects: Original Article Series, 17 (6)] (pp. 5–28). New York: Alan R. Liss.

Lindgren, S.D., Harper, D.C., & Blackman, J.A. (1986). Environmental influences and perinatal risk factors in high-risk children. *Journal of Pediatric Psychology, 11,* 531–547.

Macnab, A.J., Sheckter, L.A., Hendry, N.J., Pendray, M.R., & Macnab, G. (1985). See full citation in category C.

Mitchell, K., & Mills, N.M. (1983). Is the sensitive period in parent-infant bonding overrated? *Pediatric Nursing, 9*(2), 91–93.

Noble, D.N., & Hamilton, A.K. (1981). See full citation in category C.

Nugent, J.K. (1981). The Brazelton Neonatal Behavioral Assessment Scale: Implications for intervention. *Pediatric Nursing, 7*(3), 18–21.

O'Connor, S.M., Vietze, P.M., Sandler, H.M., Sherrod, K.B., & Altemeier, W.A. (1980). See full citation in category C.

Parmelee, A.H. (1980). Assessment of the infant at risk during the first year. In E. Sell (Ed.), *Follow-up of the high risk newborn: A practical approach* (pp. 29–41). Springfield, IL: Charles C Thomas.

Parmelee, A.H., Jr. (1985). Sensory stimulation in the nursery: How much and when? *Journal of Developmental and Behavioral Pediatrics, 6,* 242–243.

Perry, S.E. (1983). See full citation in category C.

Ramey, C.T., Zeskind, P.S., & Hunter, R.S. (1981). See full citation in category E.

Resnick, M.B., Eyler, F.D., Nelson, R.M., Eitzman, D.V., & Bucciarelli, R.L. (1987). Developmental intervention for low birth weight infants: Improved early developmental outcome. *Pediatrics, 80,* 68–74.

Riesch, S.K., & Munns, S.K. (1984). Promoting awareness: The mother and her baby. *Nursing Research, 33,* 271–276.

Sigman, M., Cohen, S.E., & Forsythe, A.B. (1981). See full citation in category E.

Taesch, H.W., & Yogman, M.W. (Eds.). (1987). *Follow-up management of the high-risk infant.* Boston: Little, Brown.

Yang, R.K. (1981). See full citation in category C.

## E.  IDENTIFICATION, ASSESSMENT, INTERVENTION

Anastasiow, N.J. (1986). See full citation in category A.

Brazelton, T.B., & Lester, B.M. (Eds.). (1984). *New approaches to developmental screening of infants.* New York: Elsevier.

Fallen, N.H., & Umansky, W. (1985). *Young children with special needs* (2nd ed.). Columbus, OH: Charles E. Merrill.

Fewell, R.R. (1983). Predicting the developmental outcome of infants at risk: Guidelines for infant assessment [From the editor]. *Topics in Early Childhood Special Education, 3*(1), viii–ix.

Gerber, M. (1984). Caring for infants with respect: The RIE approach. *Zero to Three, IX* (3), 1–3.

Gibbs, R.M. (1981). See full citation in category D.

Greenspan, S.I., Nover, R.A., Silver, B.J., & Lourie, R.S. (1979). Methodology issues and an approach to assessment in clinical infant programs. In National Institute of Mental Health, *Clinical infant intervention research programs: Selected overview and discussion* (pp. 35–45). (DHEW Publication No. ADM 79-748). Rockville, MD: Author.

Hanson, M.J. (Ed.). (1984). *Atypical infant development.* Austin, TX: PRO-ED.

Hibbs, E.D. (Ed.). (1987). *Children and families: Studies in prevention and intervention.* Madison, CT: International Universities Press.

Jordan, J.B., Gallagher, J.J., Hutinger, P., & Karnes, M.B. (Eds.). (1988). *Early childhood special education: Birth to three.* Reston, VA: Council for Exceptional Children.

Linder, T.W. (1983). *Early childhood special education: Program development and administration.* Baltimore: Paul H. Brookes Publishing Co.

Nugent, J.K. (1981). See full citation in category D.

Odom, S.L., & Karnes, M.B. (Eds.). (1988). *Early intervention for infants and children with handicaps: An empirical base.* Baltimore: Paul H. Brookes Publishing Co.

Odom, S.L., & Shuster, S.K. (1986). Handicapped children and their families. *Topics in Early Childhood Special Education, 6*(2), 68–82.

Parmelee, A.H. (1980). See full citation in category D.

Peterson, N.L. (1987). *Early intervention for handicapped and at-risk children: An introduction to early childhood special education.* Denver: Love.

Prechtl, H.F.R. (1981). Optimality: A new assessment concept.

In C.C. Brown (Ed.), *Infants at risk: Assessment and intervention* (pp. 1–5). Johnson & Johnson Baby Products Company Pediatric Round Table Series (No. 5). Somerville, NJ: Johnson & Johnson Baby Products Company.

Ramey, C.T., Zeskind, P.S., & Hunter, R.S. (1981). Biomedical and psychosocial interventions for preterm infants. In S.L. Friedman & M. Sigman (Eds.), *Preterm birth and psychological development* (pp. 395–415). San Diego: Academic Press.

Riesch, S.K., & Munns, S.K. (1984). See full citation in category D.

Schiefelbusch, R.L., & Lloyd, L.L. (Eds.). (1974). See full citation in category A.

Sheehan, R., & Keogh, B.K. (1981). Strategies for documenting progress of handicapped children in early education programs. *Educational Evaluation and Policy Analysis, 3*(6), 59–68.

Sigman, M., Cohen, S.E., & Forsythe, A.B. (1981). The relations of early infant measures to later development. In S.L. Friedman & M. Sigman (Eds.), *Preterm birth and psychological development.* San Diego: Academic Press.

Stone, N.W., & Chesney, B.H. (1978). See full citation in category A.

Ulrey, G., & Rogers, S.J. (Eds.). (1982). *Psychological assessment of handicapped infants and young children.* New York: Thieme Medical Publishers.

Wolraich, M. (1897). *The practical assessment & management of children with disorders of development and learning.* Chicago: Year Book Medical Publishers.

Woodruff, G., McGonigel, M., Garland, C.W., Zeitlin, S., Chazkel-Hochman, J., Shanahan, K., Toole, A., & Vincent, L. (1985). *Planning programs for infants.* Chapel Hill, NC: TADS, University of North Carolina. (ERIC Document Reproduction Service No. 266 573)

## F. EARLY INTERVENTION EFFICACY
(outcomes, reviews, commentaries)

Baily, E.J., & Bricker, D. (1984). The efficacy of early intervention for severely handicapped infants and young children. *Topics in Early Childhood Special Education, 4*(3), 30–51.

Barnett, W.S., & Escobar, C.M. (1988). The economics of early intervention for handicapped children: What do we really know? *Journal of the Division for Early Childhood, 12,* 169–181.

Beckman, P.J., & Burke, P.J. (1984). Early childhood special education: State of the art. *Topics in Early Childhood Special Education, 4*(1), 19–32.

Campbell, S.K. (1983). See full citation in category D.

Carta, J.J., & Greenwood, C.R. (1985). Eco-behavioral assessment: A methodology for expanding the evaluation of early intervention programs. *Topics in Early Childhood Special Education, 5*(2), 88–104.

Casto, G., Ascione, F., & Salehi, M. (Eds.). (1987). *Current perspectives in infancy and early childhood research.* Logan: Utah State University, Early Intervention Research Institute Press.

Casto, G., & Lewis, A. (1986). Selecting outcome measures in early intervention. *Journal of the Division for Early Childhood, 10,* 118–123.

Casto, G., & Mastropieri, M.A. (1986). The efficacy of early intervention programs: A meta-analysis. *Exceptional Children, 52,* 417–424.

*Charting change in infants, families and services: A guide to program evaluation for administrators and practitioners.* (1987). Washington, DC: National Center for Clinical Infant Programs.

Cohen, S.E., Parmelee, A.H., Beckwith, L., & Sigman, M. (1986). Cognitive development in preterm infants: Birth to 8 years. *Journal of Developmental and Behavioral Pediatrics, 7,* 102–110.

Dunst, C.J. (1985). Rethinking early intervention. *Analysis and Intervention in Developmental Disabilities, 5,* 165–201.

Dunst, C.J. (1986). Overview of the efficacy of early intervention programs: Methodological and conceptual considerations. In L. Bickman & D. Weatherford (Eds.), *Evaluating early intervention programs for severely handicapped children and their families* (pp. 79–147). Austin, TX: PRO-ED.

Gallagher, J.J., & Ramey, C.T. (1987). See full citation in category A.

Garwood, S.G. (Ed.). (1983). *Educating young handicapped children: A developmental approach.* (2nd ed.). Rockville, MD: Aspen Publishers.

Greenspan, S.I., & White, K.R. (1985). The efficacy of preventive intervention: A glass half full? *Zero to Three, V*(1), 1–5.

Greenspan, S.I., & White, K.R. (1987). Conducting research with preventive intervention programs. In I.F. Berlin & J. Noshpitz (Eds.), *Basic handbook of child psychiatry* (pp. 554–565). New York: Basic Books.

Hanson, M.J. (1985). An analysis of the effects of early intervention services for infants and toddlers with moderate and severe handicaps. *Topics in Early Childhood Special Education, 5*(2), 36–51.

Harris, S.R. (1988). Early intervention: Does developmental therapy make a difference? *Topics in Early Childhood Special Education, 7*(4), 20–32.

Provence, S. (1985). On the efficacy of early intervention programs. *Journal of Developmental and Behavioral Pediatrics 6,* 363–366.

Rosenberg, S.A., Robinson, C.C., Finkler, D., & Rose, J.S. (1987). An empirical comparison of formulas evaluating early intervention program impact on development. *Exceptional Children, 54,* 213–219.

Russel, F.F. (1985). See full citation in category C.

Shonkoff, J.P. (1984). A critical look at early intervention programs for developmentally vulnerable infants [Abstract]. *Journal of Developmental and Behavioral Pediatrics, 5,* 150–151.

White, K.R., Bush, D.W., & Casto, G.C. (1986). Learning from reviews of early intervention. *Journal of Special Education, 19,* 417–428.

White, K.R., & Casto, G. (1985). An integrative review of early intervention efficacy studies with at-risk children: Implications for the handicapped. *Analysis and Intervention in Developmental Disabilities, 5,* 7–31.

White, K.R., & Mott, S.E. (1987). Conducting longitudinal research on the efficacy of early intervention with handicapped children. *Journal of the Division for Early Childhood, 12,* 13–22.

## G.  PARENT AUTHORS

Jablow, M.M. (1982). *Cara: Growing with a retarded child.* Philadelphia: Temple University Press.

Massie, R., & Massie, S. (1975). *Journey.* New York: Delacorte Press.

Murray, J.B., & Murray, E. (1975). *And say what he is: The life of a special child.* Cambridge, MA: MIT Press.

Simons, R. (1987). *After the tears.* San Diego, CA: Harcourt Brace Jovanovich.

## H.  POLICY

Barnett, W.S. (1986). Methodological issues in economic evaluation of early intervention programs. *Early Childhood Research Quarterly, 1,* 249–268.

Barnett, W.S. (1988). The economics of preschool special education under Public Law 99-457. *Topics in Early Childhood Special Education, 8*(1), 12–23.

Blendon, R.J., & Altman, D.E. (1984). Public attitudes about health care costs: A lesson in national schizophrenia [Special report]. *New England Journal of Medicine, 311,* 613–616.

Cena, S., & Caro, F.G. (1984). *Supporting families who care for severely disabled children at home: A public policy perspective.* New York: Community Services Society of New York.

Garwood, S.G. (1987). Political, economic, and practical issues affecting the development of universal early intervention for handicapped infants. *Topics in Early Childhood Special Education, 7*(2), 6–18.

Hayes, C. (Ed.). (1982). *Making policies for children: A study of the federal process.* Washington, DC: National Academy Press.

Perlmutter, M. (Ed.). (1983). *Development and policy concerning children with special needs.* Minnesota Symposium on Child Psychology, Vol. 16. Hillsdale, NJ: Lawrence Erlbaum Associates.

Schorr, L.B. (1988). *Within our reach: Breaking the cycle of disadvantage.* New York: Doubleday.

White, K.R. (1988). See full citation in category B.

Zigler, E.F. (1983, December). *How to impact social policy affecting children and families.* Paper presented at the Third Biennial Training Institute of the National Center for Clinical Infant Programs, Washington, DC.

Zigler, E.F., & Finn, M. (1982). A vision of child care in the 1980's. In L. Bond & J. Joffe (Eds.), *Facilitating infant and early childhood development* (pp. 443–465). Hanover, NH: University of New England Press.

## I. OTHER

Badger, E., & Burns, D. (1982). A model for coalescing birth-to-three programs. In L. Bond & J. Joffe (Eds.), *Facilitating infant and early childhood development* (pp. 513–537). Hanover, NH: University of New England Press.

Bailey, D.B., Farel, A.M., O'Donnell, K.J, Simeonsson, R.J., &

Miller, C.A. (1986). Preparing infant interventionists: Inter-departmental training in special education and maternal and child health. *Journal of the Division for Early Childhood, 11,* 67–77.

Batshaw, M.L., & Perret, Y.M. (1986). *Children with handicaps: A medical primer* (2nd ed.). Baltimore: Paul H. Brookes Publishing Co.

Blacher, J. (Ed.). (1984). *Severely handicapped young children and their families: Research in review.* San Diego: Academic Press.

Blackman, J.A. (Ed.). (1984). *Medical aspects of developmental disabilities in children birth to three.* Rockville, MD: Aspen Publishers.

Blackman, J.A., & Healy, A. (1983). *The needs of children with cerebral palsy: A comprehensive view.* Iowa City: The University of Iowa.

*Clinical infant intervention research programs: Selected overview and discussion.* See National Institute of Mental Health, 1979.

Connolly, J.A., & Cullen, J.H. (1983). Maternal stress and the origins of health status. In J.D. Call, E. Galenson, & R.L. Tyson (Eds.), *Frontiers of infant psychiatry* (pp. 273–281). New York: Basic Books.

Donabedian, A. (1980). *Explorations in quality assessment and monitoring: Vol. 1. The definition of quality and approaches to its assessment.* Ann Arbor, MI: Health Administration Press.

Fein, G.G. (1981). The physical environment: Stimulation or evocation. In R.M. Lerner & N.A. Busch-Rossnagel (Eds.), *Individuals as producers of their development: A life-span perspective* (pp. 257–279). San Diego: Academic Press.

Garbarino, J., Brookhouser, P.E., Authier, K.J., & Associates. (1987). *Special children, special risks: The maltreatment of children with disabilities.* New York: Aldine De Gruyter.

Gilkerson, L., Hilliard, A.G., III, Schrag, E., & Shonkoff, J.

(1987). *Report accompanying the education of the Handicapped Act Amendments (Report #99-860) and commenting on Public Law 99-457.* (Available from the National Center for Clinical Infant Programs, 733 15th Street, N.W., Washington, DC).

Green, M., Ferry, P.C., Russman, B.S., Shonkoff, J.P., & Taft, L.T. (1987). Early intervention programs: Where do pediatricians fit in? [Symposium]. *Contemporary Pediatrics, 5*(3), 92–118.

Guralnick, M.J., Bennett, F.C., Heiser, K.E., Richardson, B., Jr., & Shibley R.E., Jr. (1987). Training residents in developmental pediatrics: Results from a national replication. *Journal of Developmental and Behavioral Pediatrics, 8,* 260–265.

Jackson, E. (1982). Environments of high-risk and handicapped infants. In C.T. Ramey & P.L. Trohanis (Eds.), *Finding and educating high-risk and handicapped infants* (pp. 53–67). Austin, TX: PRO-ED.

Jens, K.G., & O'Donnell, K.E. (1982). Bridging the gap between research and intervention with handicapped infants. In D.D. Bricker (Ed.), *Intervention with at-risk and handicapped infants: From research to application* (pp. 31–43). Austin, TX: PRO-ED.

Jones, S.N., & Meisels, S.J. (1987). Training family day care providers to work with special needs children. *Topics in Early Childhood Special Education, 7*(1), 1–12.

Khan, N.A., & Battle, C.U. (1987). Chronic illness: Implications for development and education. *Topics in Early Childhood Special Education, 6*(4), 25–32.

Kisker, C.T. (1983). *The needs of children with cancer: A comprehensive view.* Iowa City: The University of Iowa.

Kopp, C.B. (1982). The role of theoretical frameworks in the study of at-risk and handicapped young children. In D.D. Bricker (Ed.), *Intervention with at-risk and handicapped infants: From research to application* (pp. 13–30). Austin, TX: PRO-ED.

Levine, M.D., Carey, W.B, Crocker, A.C., & Gross, R.T. (Eds.). (1983). *Developmental-behavioral pediatrics*. Philadelphia: W.B. Saunders.

Mather, J., & Weinstein, E. (1988). Teachers and therapists: Evolution of a partnership in early intervention. *Topics in Early Childhood Special Education, 7*(4), 1–9.

McAfee, J.K. (1987). Integrating therapy services in the school: A model for training educators, administrators, and therapists. *Topics in Early Childhood Special Education, 7*(3), 116–126.

McCollum, J.A. (1987). Early interventionists in infant and early childhood programs: A comparison of preservice training needs. *Topics in Early Childhood Special Education, 7*(3), 24–35.

Miller, C.A., Coulter, E.J., Fine, A., Adams-Taylor, S., & Schorr, L.B. (1985). 1984 update on the world economic crisis and the children: A United States case study. *International Journal of Health Services, 15*, 431–450.

Miller, C.A., Fine, A., Adams-Taylor, S., & Schorr, L.B. (1986). *Monitoring children's health: Key indicators*. Washington, DC: American Public Health Association.

Morris, H. (1983). *The needs of children with cleft lip and palate: A comprehensive view*. Iowa City: The University of Iowa.

National Institute of Mental Health. (1979). *Clinical infant intervention research programs: Selected overview and discussion* (DHEW Publication No. ADM 79-748). Rockville, MD: Author.

Osofsky, H.J., & Osofsky, J.D. (1980). Normal adaptation to pregnancy and new parenthood. In P.M. Taylor (Ed.), *Parent-infant relationships* (pp. 25–48). Orlando: Grune & Stratton.

*Report of the Surgeon General's workshop on children with handicaps and their families*. See U.S. Department of Health and Human Services, 1983.

Rustia, J., & Barr, L. (1985). Wanted: More health services in early intervention programs. *American Journal of Maternal/Child Nursing (MCN), 10,* 260–264.

Schorr, L.B. (1983). Environmental deterrents: Poverty, affluence, violence, and television. In M.D. Levine, W.B. Carey, A.C. Crocker, & R.T. Gross (Eds.), *Developmental-behavioral pediatrics* (pp. 293–312). Philadelphia: W.B. Saunders.

Shonkoff, J.P. (1981). *Changing concepts of infancy in American society: Implications for developmental assessment and early intervention programs in the first three years of life.* Report to W.K. Kellogg Foundation, Battle Creek, MI.

Shore, M.F. (1981). Marking time in the land of plenty: Reflections on mental health in the United States. *American Journal of Orthopsychiatry, 51,* 391–402.

START (State Technical Assistance Resource Team). See *The 1986–87 handicapped children's early education program directory* (1987).

Trohanis, P.L. (1985). Designing a plan for in-service education. *Topics in Early Childhood Special Education, 5*(1), 63–82.

U.S. Department of Health and Human Services. (1983). *Report of the Surgeon General's workshop on children with handicaps and their families* (DHHS Publication No. PHS 83-50194). Washington, DC: U.S. Government Printing Office.

Werner, E.E. (1984). Vulnerable, but invincible children [Abstract]. *Journal of Developmental and Behavioral Pediatrics, 5,* 145.

Wolraich, M. (1983). *The needs of children with spina bifida: A comprehensive view.* Iowa City: The University of Iowa.

Wolraich, M., & Siperstein, G.N. (1983). Assessing professionals' prognostic impressions of mental retardation. *Mental Retardation, 21,* 8–12.

Zigler, E., & Berman, W. (1983). Discerning the future of early childhood intervention. *American Psychologist, 38,* 894–906.

# Index

225